Contents

Editor's Preface

SINCE 1968, when the Economic History Society and Macmillan published the first of the 'Studies in Economic and Social History', the series has established itself as a major teaching tool in universities, colleges and schools, and as a familiar landmark in serious bookshops throughout the country. A great deal of the credit for this must go to the wise leadership of its first editor, Professor M. W. Flinn, who retired at the end of 1977. The books tend to be bigger now than they were originally, and inevitably more expensive; but they have continued to provide information in modest compass at a reasonable price by the standards of modern academic publications.

There is no intention of departing from the principles of the first decade. Each book aims to survey findings and discussion in an important field of economic or social history that has been the subject of recent lively debate. It is meant as an introduction for readers who are not themselves professional researchers but who want to know what the discussion is all about – students, teachers and others generally interested in the subject. The authors, rather than either taking a strongly partisan line or suppressing their own critical faculties, set out the arguments and the problems as fairly as they can, and attempt a critical summary and explanation of them from their own judgement. The discipline now embraces so wide a field in the study of the human past that it would be inappropriate for each book to follow an identical plan, but all volumes will normally contain an extensive descriptive bibliography.

The series is not meant to provide all the answers but to help readers to see the problems clearly enough to form their own conclusions. We shall never agree in history, but the discipline will be well served if we know what we are disagreeing about, and why.

T. C. SMOUT

University of St Andrews   *Editor*

STUDIES IN ECONOMIC AND SOCIAL HISTORY

This series, specially commissioned by the Economic History Society, provides a guide to the current interpretations of the key themes of economic and social history in which advances have recently been made or in which there has been significant debate.

Originally entitled 'Studies in Economic History', in 1974 the series had its scope extended to include topics in social history, and the new series title, 'Studies in Economic and Social History', signalises this development.

The series gives readers access to the best work done, helps them to draw their own conclusions in major fields of study, and by means of the critical bibliography in each book guides them in the selection of further reading. The aim is to provide a springboard to further work rather than a set of pre-packaged conclusions or short-cuts.

ECONOMIC HISTORY SOCIETY

The Economic History Society, which numbers over 3000 members, publishes the *Economic History Review* four times a year (free to members) and holds an annual conference. Enquiries about membership should be addressed to the Assistant Secretary, Economic History Society, Peterhouse, Cambridge. Full-time students may join at special rates.

STUDIES IN ECONOMIC AND SOCIAL HISTORY

Edited for the Economic History Society by T. C. Smout

PUBLISHED

OTHER TITLES ARE IN PREPARATION

Britain in Tropical Africa, 1880–1960
Economic Relationships and Impact

J. FORBES MUNRO

Senior Lecturer,
Department of Economic History
University of Glasgow

MACMILLAN PRESS
LONDON

First published 1984 by
THE MACMILLAN PRESS LTD
London and Basingstoke
Companies and representatives
throughout the world

Typeset by
Wessex Typesetters Ltd
Frome, Somerset
Printed in Hong Kong

British Library Cataloguing in Publication Data
Munro, J. Forbes
Britain in tropical Africa, 1880–1960.–(Studies
in economic and social history)
1. Africa–Economic conditions   2. Great
Britain–Colonies–Africa
I. Title   II. Series
330.96'03   HC502
ISBN 0–333–32330–0

Introduction

THIS pamphlet is intended as an addition to the group of pamphlets within the series which deals with the less developed parts of the world and their relations with the advanced industrial economies. More specifically, it is seen as complementing two earlier contributions, by P. J. Cain on Britain's overseas expansion and by N. Charlesworth on British rule in India. Readers should be aware of the limitations of the present essay. It is concerned primarily with the economic consequences of British colonialism in Africa, and therefore cannot be regarded as a fully comprehensive discussion of modern African economic history. Little account has been taken of pre-colonial conditions, for example, and a number of themes of interest to Africanists – notably ecological and demographic issues – are given less weight than they might otherwise merit. Nor has it been possible to deal with the transfer of power at the end of the colonial period. Nevertheless, it is hoped that the pamphlet deals with a sufficiently broad range of topics and debates to satisfy students both of Britain's 'imperial economy' and of African economic history.

My thanks go to Professors T. C. Smout and A. G. Hopkins for their encouragement and advice, and to Professor Cyril Ehrlich for his helpful comments. Mrs Blythe O'Driscoll, Mrs Linda Craig and Mrs Edna Dorrington typed the manuscript most efficiently while dealing with all the other demands of a busy departmental office.

Note on References

References in the text within square brackets relate to the numbered items in the Select Bibliography, followed, where necessary, by the page numbers in italics, for example: [5: 27].

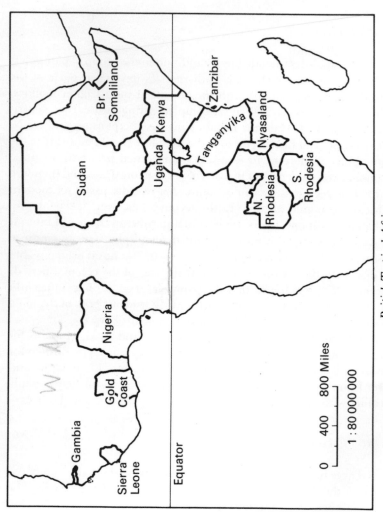

British Tropical Africa

1 Themes and Approaches

TROPICAL Africa, the lands lying between the Sahara desert and the Limpopo river, sometimes also regarded as 'Black Africa' between the Arab North and the white-ruled South, historically experienced both governance by British agencies and penetration by British business. Trade and investment, however, were never wholly synonymous with, or dependent upon, the exercise of colonial administration. British capitalism's links with the coastal areas of West Africa originated long before the colonial Partition of the 1880s and 1890s. British merchants and financiers subsequently participated in the economic activity of Belgian, Portuguese, French and German, as well as British, colonial territories. The retreat from formal empire during the late 1950s and the 1960s left British business interests to operate under local African governments once again. The economic connections between Britain and Tropical Africa, in short, were wider and more enduring than those relationships with territories under British sovereignty. But if colonialism and capitalism did not always require each other's support, the central thrust of Britain's economic impact on Tropical Africa took place between 1880 and 1960 in what were, or became, formal dependencies.

Compared with a presence of some four centuries in the Caribbean, or two centuries of dominance in India, British rule in Tropical Africa had a relatively short life-span. Apart from a few settlements along the west coast, founded in the days of the Atlantic slave trade or its abolition, formal sovereignty lasted for little more than eighty or ninety years. But Britain's colonial possessions in West, East and Central Africa, acquired at the height of its industrial and political power, made up a considerable part of the 'dependent empire' and therefore loom large in the literature on British imperialism in the Third World. They comprised fourteen colonial territories, of varying sizes and differing constitutional links with the Crown. The Gambia, Sierra Leone, the Gold Coast (now Ghana) and Nigeria constituted British West Africa. Kenya, Uganda and Zanzibar, together with

Tanganyika which was taken over from Germany after the First World War, were what became conventionally known as British East Africa, but a wider definition would include British Somaliland and the Anglo-Egyptian Sudan. The latter, theoretically a condominium shared with Egypt, was in practice ruled by Britain (although administratively separate from the Colonial Office). Finally, the territories of Southern Rhodesia (Zimbabwe), Northern Rhodesia (Zambia) and Nyasaland (Malawi) collectively comprised British Central Africa. The two Rhodesias were governed by a chartered company, the British South Africa Company, until the early 1920s, when the European population of Southern Rhodesia obtained internal self-government and Northern Rhodesia came under the Colonial Office. British Tropical Africa was even less of a unified, coherent entity than British India, and discussion of its economic history needs to take account of differences between, and within, the three principal regions. Nevertheless, amidst the diversity there are also certain common themes which derive from the shared experience of rule by Britain and interaction with the British economy.

Economic historians have been engaged in exploring two principal aspects of that relationship – first, the nature of the connections between Britain and Africa, that is their origins, extent and causes, and second, the effects of the British presence on economic life in Africa. But the latter has provoked by far the greater controversy.

In what ways, and why, were material conditions and economic institutions transformed under colonial rule? Who benefited from these changes and by how much? Was the economic impact on Africa wholesome or malign? On such questions no clear consensus has emerged and the last one is particularly contentious, raising as it does yet a further issue – what is the appropriate yardstick by which economic change in colonial Africa may be judged? Is it in terms of economic growth and welfare, as conventionally measured by increases in per capita output and improvements in real incomes over time? Or in terms of the creation of economic conditions conducive to political independence, national self-reliance and self-respect? Or in terms of historical materialism, the development of modes of production leading to class struggle, and the potential for a 'transition to socialism'? Disagreement over the historical record, as well as a great deal of confusion of purpose, has arisen from the interplay between these very different approaches to evaluation of the past.

The pioneering academic assessments, appearing between the two

World Wars, when colonialism was firmly established and at its most secure, emphasised the activities of British administrators, businessmen and settlers in 'opening-up' Tropical Africa to imperial and international trade, and in creating a 'monetary economy' in regions assumed to be dominated by subsistence production and barter exchange. Pre-colonial history was largely ignored and Africans tended to be depicted as passive participants in processes of economic transformation initiated and controlled by the outsiders. Thus, for McPhee in 1926 [109], 'economic revolution' in West Africa meant the growth of foreign trade consequent upon the introduction of colonial law and order, the development of modern transport and improvements in public health. Hancock, with his identification and exploration of the distinction between settlers' and traders' frontiers [37], carried the interpretation of Britain's economic role in Africa to more sophisticated levels but still remained essentially within the 'imperial tradition' of historiography. This perspective, expressing admiration for what was seen as the positive achievements of colonial rule, gradually lost popularity after the Second World War but did not completely disappear from view. It supplied, for example, much of the vigour with which Gann and Duignan defend European colonialism in Africa, reasserting its role as a 'liberating force' in a backward and largely stagnant continent. 'The European rulers', Gann and Duignan state,

> did provide the basic infrastructure for Black Africa; they encouraged mining and mineral industries, plantation and peasant farming for export. They began secondary industrial growth. The colonists also built the support services of education, social services and government research necessary for future growth. The European administrators and their ancillary agents – European missionaries, businessmen and technicians – introduced new skills and new occupations and created many new needs. The colonial period thus forced Africa into the modern world economy; colonialism supplied the engines for progress and modernization. [2: *693*; 3]

The power of that engine and the direction of its thrust, however, were questioned by the 'liberal wave' of economic historians whose scholarship came to the fore coincidentally with, or hard on the heels of, the retreat of British authority from Africa in the early 1960s. The work of Ehrlich [89; 90; 35; 91], Wrigley [187; 124; 125; 126], Hopkins

11

[4], Hill [151; 152], Gray and Birmingham [224] and others challenged the 'imperial tradition' at a number of points. By investigating pre-colonial patterns of production and exchange they demonstrated that the market economy in Tropical Africa – especially in the West but also in the East – had antecedents pre-dating the arrival of European rule, and that a basic continuity of innovation and receptivity to change, both in commerce and in agriculture, carried through from the pre-colonial to the colonial era. It was established that much of the spread of cash-cropping which occurred in the late nineteenth and early twentieth centuries was the product of African enterprise, owing little or nothing to direct assistance from the colonial government. When seen against the longer-term history of agrarian societies, colonial rule could no longer be assumed to provide the only dynamic for change or the only source of 'progress' in post-1870 Africa. Nor could it be assumed that the power of colonial government was invariably or inexorably exercised in the pursuit of growth and welfare, for it was frequently used to intervene in or regulate market relationships in ways which could be held to distort the 'natural' tendencies of the economic system. Finally, the extent to which British colonial authorities possessed either the will or the means to transform African economies and societies came to be questioned. In Ehrlich's view, the administrators were 'caretakers' rather than 'builders', concerned to maintain the status quo rather than to promote radical change [35]. In short, 'the colonial era has ceased to be regarded as the sole substance of African history, and there are sound reasons for thinking that colonial rule itself had a less dramatic and less pervasive economic impact than was once supposed' [13: *167*]. But although the liberals qualified and modified the older imperial perspective, broadly in tune with the reformist mood of the 1950s and 1960s, they did not wholly depart from a view of the colonial period as one of positive achievement and real gains. They might argue that more could and should have been done by the colonial authorities but would probably agree that 'there is plenitude of evidence of material progress in Africa between 1870 and 1960. . . . And extraordinary feats of imagination are needed to avoid the admission that colonialism was instrumental in these changes' [16: *270*].

To members of the 'dependency' or 'development of under-development' school of thought, however, such a conclusion is either erroneous or irrelevant. Application of 'dependency' theory to

African economic history, according to Alpers, one of its exponents [7: *164*], was rooted in the political and economic failures of many African states during the first decade of independence. It was therefore profoundly teleological in its orientation, using history to explain the inability of a political leadership to deliver immediate and dramatic material improvement. Drawing inspiration from Latin American structuralists, in particular A. G. Frank, a succession of Africanists, including Amin [8; 79], Rodney [6], Alpers [222] and Leys [102], contributed to the emergence of an interpretation of African history which stressed domination and exploitation by European capitalism – from the slave trade and pre-colonial commodity trades, through the period of formal colonialism into the recent years of political independence. Turning the precepts of the 'imperial tradition' upsidedown, they argued that colonialism 'underdeveloped' Africa by opening it up to fuller penetration by Western capitalism. Capitalism in turn sucked surpluses from Africa by way of 'unequal exchange' and remittance of profits – an echo here of the drain thesis of Indian economic history – and structured African economies and societies into an externally-oriented and self-perpetuating dependence. Over-reliance on primary product exporting, limited industrialisation and pronounced socio-economic inequalities became the hallmarks of economies which were rendered peripheral to industrial capitalism and thus transformed from an *un*developed to an *under*developed condition. For the neo-Marxists of the 'dependency' school, 'the operation of the imperialist system bears major responsibility for African economic retardation by draining African wealth and by making it impossible to develop more rapidly the resources of the continent' [6: *237*].

The debate which followed the appearance of 'dependency' in the study of Africa has been conducted largely at a theoretical level, with only a limited use of concrete historical evidence or case-study. The approach has been attacked in its turn for its apparent lack of interest in the question as to whether material conditions actually improved or not in colonial Africa, for its tendency to define 'underdevelopment' tautologously as 'dependence', and for its assumption that trade is a zero-sum game in which one party gains while the other loses [10; 11]. Perhaps the most vigorous counter-thrust, however, has come from scholars working within the Marxist paradigm, for whom relationships of production are of greater analytical significance than exchange relationships. Starting from Marx's formulation of the function of capitalism in the Third World as being to erode non-capitalist social formations and then regenerate them as 'bourgeois' ones, that is to play an historically 'progressive' role, they deny that external capitalism either effectively penetrated Africa during the colonial era or transformed its dominant modes of production into capitalist ones. This absence of a truly significant impact, first argued by Brett [88], is explained by Kay as a consequence of the fact that, at least until the Second World War, Africa and the rest of the Third World experienced the activities of 'merchant' capital rather than 'industrial' capital, and that 'merchant' capital, 'despite its corrosive effects, has bolstered up archaic political and economic forms through a series of alliances with powerful elements in the pre-capitalist orders' [13: *104*]. Some attempt has been made to absorb this viewpoint within a basic 'dependency' approach. Howard, for example, has argued that 'underdevelopment' in Ghana resulted from the fact that 'it was not in the interests of the core capitalist nations to allow capitalism to develop completely' [96: *25*], but such a reformulation receives no support from Hyden, for whom the interest of Western capitalism *requires* the replacement of pre-capitalist modes of production by more efficient ones. This did not occur, he asserts, because there were barriers to capitalist expansion within Third World countries [97: *22*].

For at least one strand of thought within the Marxist framework, therefore, Western capitalism in Tropical Africa was weak and ineffective, unable to achieve 'revolutionary' change. In this it mirrors some of the liberal conclusions about Western colonialism. Indeed, the 'orthodox' or 'classical' Marxist position seems to share with the liberal approach a characteristic which distinguishes them from both the 'imperial' and 'dependency' schools – namely an insistence that evaluation of the economic and social consequences of colonial rule requires as much attention to be paid to internally-located dynamics and statics as to externally-derived ones. What Britain, or Europe, or the world economy did to Africa is only part of the story of Africa's recent economic past.

2 Origins of British Rule

WHY did Britain acquire a scattering of colonial possessions in Tropical Africa, annexing new territories and enlarging existing ones during the last quarter of the nineteenth century? What was the extent and nature of the interplay between colonialism and capitalism (or government and business) in the initial emergence of British rule? Such questions have long fascinated historians, not least because of the need to fit Africa into general explanations of European overseas expansion and because of the connection with debates over theories of imperialism.

The wider background to Britain's involvement with the less-developed world has been dealt with in another contribution to this pamphlet series [19] and need not be repeated here. For Africa, the most relevant context is the changing character of the international economy after 1870 or so, with the diffusion of industrialism beyond Britain generating more intense competition for markets, and the effects of these developments upon the European state system [5: *64–85*]. In contrast to monocausal explanations of Britain's annex-ationist appetite which stress the primacy of such factors as a propensity to export surplus capital or a pre-emptive staking of claims to raw material supplies [33], there have emerged assessments which emphasise the complexity of Britain's political economy at the time and identify several influences on policy-makers. Britain's relative industrial weakness after 1870, which led to a more aggressive search for markets, a continuing financial expansion and emergent inter-national competition for overseas investment opportunities, and the challenge of German imperial expansion, all disposed Whitehall and Westminster to look more favourably than hitherto on fresh colonial annexations [20: *484–9*]. Where and how such general tendencies were transformed into concrete reality, however, depended upon the specific overseas location of established and emergent economic interests. Such interest groups might be domestic or more broadly imperial in character.

In West Africa, for example, a direct British commercial connection already existed in 1880. This linked Merseyside and Lancashire to indigenous African economies through a modest exchange of manufactures, especially cotton textiles, for raw materials, especially vegetable oils. Regular steamshipping connections had been established, notably by Elder Dempster & Co. of Liverpool [51; 53]. Political and administrative support for such activities was present in the coastal areas of the Gambia, Sierra Leone, the Gold Coast and Lagos Protectorate, and was informally exercised in the Niger Delta. The transformation of this fairly limited presence into full-scale colonial sovereignty, and more especially the extension of British authority over what became the Federation of Nigeria, was partly a defensive measure, designed to protect areas of mercantile endeavour, as well as actual or potential markets for British goods, from French or German encroachment. The Lancashire lobby was sensitive at this time to threats to its markets for cotton goods [26]. But colonial expansion in the region was also in part an attempt to reduce or restrain the competition which had developed in the palm oil trades from the 1870s, as a result of declining commodity prices and a shift in the terms of trade against West African producers [4: 124–66; 25]. Although doubts have been expressed about the extent to which traders' reactions to the commercial 'crisis' actually influenced metropolitan decision-taking [18], as well as the relevance of this factor to colonial expansion outside the palm oil belt, the insecurity of the British merchants undoubtedly played a significant part in events. It resulted in conflict with African middlemen, pressures for combination and merger among the mercantile houses, and demand for support from chambers of commerce and governments [30]. Problems were most pronounced on the Niger River, where Sir George Goldie obtained administrative powers for his Royal Niger Company and successfully defended a monopsony which rendered the firm profitable through the years of trade depression [22; 28]. The protection and promotion of existing mercantile interests, and to a lesser extent manufacturing interests, figured prominently in the making of Britain's colonial empire in West Africa.

By contrast, there existed in 1880 virtually no direct commercial relationship between Britain and East or Central Africa. Consequently, economic motivations for colonial annexations in these regions were rather more imperial and financial than metropolitan and commercial. The aspirations of business groups based in South

Africa and India, but with financial ties to the City of London, became intertwined with the British government's strategic concern for the imperial sea-routes around the Cape and through Suez [31] and together supplied the driving-force behind the penetration and conquest of territories as yet little involved in world trade but regarded as possible fields for colonisation and investment.

Real estate speculation was perhaps strongest in the northern thrust of the Cape Colony interests associated with Cecil Rhodes. This may be seen as a search for compensation for Rhodes' belated and initially unsuccessful investment in the gold-fields of the Witwatersrand [29], or can be interpreted more broadly as the 'sub-imperialism' of a Cape society which was developing its own 'colonial capitalism' and expansionary instincts [32; 27]. In the aftermath of the Rand discoveries a rush for mineral and land concessions across the Limpopo in Mashonaland and Matabeleland, and then north across the Zambezi as far as the copper-bearing country of Katanga (Shaba), was led by the British South Africa Company. The mining-settler frontier supplied the economic foundations of what became Southern and Northern Rhodesia, and had a bearing upon the acquisition of the Central Africa (latterly Nyasaland) Protectorate [24]. In the latter territory the advancing Cape interests rubbed up against a lesser stream of Natal expansionism which was probing commercial prospects northwards along the Indian Ocean coastline, seeking out possible sources of labour for Natal's plantations as well as highland areas for further white colonisation [21]. This overlapped in turn with the advance into East Africa of William Mackinnon's India-based network of steam-shipping and trade. Mackinnon's territorial ambitions in East Africa, initially limited in scope, less than single-mindedly pursued, and potentially far less profitable than those of Rhodes in Central Africa, were at first resisted by Whitehall, which preferred 'informal' influence through the Sultan of Zanzibar, but they were revived and enlarged in the mid-1880s as a counter-weight to an unexpected German intervention in the region. While the Imperial British East Africa Company enjoyed little success as a trading concern it secured British sovereignty over Uganda and what became Kenya Colony and Protectorate [23].

Only in the Upper Nile basin, in what became the Anglo-Egyptian Sudan, did colonialism establish itself ahead of a capitalist probing of the resources and market potential of the area. Here the strategic

17

defence of the Suez Canal seemed to demand a British military and administrative presence in a territory with little immediate commercial or financial attraction. Otherwise, the frontiers of the British state and the frontiers of the 'imperial economy' advanced into Tropical Africa together, the one sometimes ahead of the other but with the bureaucrat and businessman generally recognising and responding to each other's needs.

There were, however, regional divergences in the patterns of business activity and relationships, reflecting perhaps a dichotomy alleged to exist within the British economy itself. West Africa's external economic connections were principally oriented towards Britain's industrial north-west, while the emergent relationships of East and Central Africa were with centres of mercantile-financial operation elsewhere in the Empire and through them to the City of London. The merchants and industrialists of Liverpool and Manchester regarded Africa in terms of markets for manufactures, sources of industrial raw materials, and profits from the immediate exchange of such goods. London and 'imperial' capital tended to see Africa as land to be possessed, settled and exploited, to yield a return in rent, royalties or interest, or as commodities to be traded throughout the world economy. Such distinctions, while they would erode through time, lasted well into the colonial period itself [58: 274–5].

3 Trade, Investment and Expatriate Business

BRITAIN acquired colonial possessions in Tropical Africa for essentially defensive reasons: to ensure, in the face of the neo-mercantilist tendencies of other European states, that some parts of the African continent would remain open to British trade and investment. For a Britain committed to free trade at home and abroad, the ideal colony was an open economy, actively engaged in world trade through the exporting of agricultural and mineral products and importing of manufactures [4: *168–72*]. Economic growth would occur as the natural outcome of interaction between private interests, British and local, and as a spontaneous consequence of comparative advantage in production for world markets. There should therefore be minimal restrictions on the movement of commodities, capital or labour.

[margin note: HOPKINS "EC HISTORY OF W. AF"]

The primacy of this model lasted in British thought until the 1930s, and substantially beyond, so that for most of the period of colonial rule Africa was not thirled to Britain by any tariff system designed to protect or promote British or imperial trade. The exceptions, when Britain's colonial trade policy acquired a tinge of mercantilism, came relatively late and lasted a relatively short time. In the 1930s Britain imposed imperial preferences on Gambia and Sierra Leone, and introduced textile import quotas in Nigeria and the Gold Coast, and during the Second World War physical and price controls were exercised over British Tropical Africa's external trade. These lingered into the post-war years but were dismantled again by the early 1950s.

Currency was perhaps a stronger bond between colony and metropolis than trade restrictions. With colonial rule there arrived new currencies – British in West Africa, Indian in East Africa and South African in Central Africa – to replace the variety of local, indigenous units of value. Private banks issued notes. In time, however, currency boards were set up in London for each region – West Africa in 1912, East Africa in 1919 and Central Africa in 1940 –

to issue local currency backed by holdings of British government securities. The timing and reasons for change were specific to each region [39; 130: *281–7*], but the general result was to bring all the currencies of British Tropical Africa into a relationship of free convertibility with sterling. While this encouraged trade between Britain and Africa, the effect was especially marked between the mid-1930s and mid-1950s when, with Britain once again off the Gold Standard and acting as the centre of a sterling trade bloc, there was a lack of convertibility between sterling and other major world currencies [36: *606–8*; 44].

Table I British Tropical Africa: Exports and Imports by Value
(£ million, current prices. Five-year averages)

	West		East[a]		Central	
	Exports	Imports	Exports	Imports	Exports	Imports
1890–94	2.5	2.4	–	–	–	–
1895–99	3.5	3.3	1.8	2.1	n.a.	n.a.
1900–04	4.2	5.2	1.6	2.0	n.a.	1.6
1905–09	6.8	7.8	2.4	4.3	2.7	2.0
1910–14	12.9	13.4	4.0	5.8	3.5	3.3
1915–19	18.2	15.3	7.8	10.4	5.1	3.5
1920–24	23.4	26.4	11.5	15.7	4.5	5.5
1925–29	30.8	28.4	16.7	21.3	4.8	10.1
1930–34	17.8	14.5	11.5	13.7	5.5	9.4
1935–39	23.3	24.1	17.3	18.9	13.4	12.6
1940–44	21.7	23.1	23.3	26.9	21.7	17.1
1945–49	76.7	53.9	54.7	67.8	41.7	48.7
1950–54	217.7	173.9	140.3	152.3	121.0	112.6
1955–59	244.9	278.7	175.9	193.8	166.7	156.6

[a] Excludes Tanganyika before 1920.

Sources: *Statistical Abstracts for the British Empire/Commonwealth* (various issues); *UN Statistical Yearbook* (1961).

Free trade backed by a sound currency was Britain's prescription for colonial Africa. The growth of trade which occurred within this system is indicated by Table I. Although rates of increase were high by international standards, they began from an initially very low level

20

of participation in world trade. The West African pattern was that of a gradual build-up of external trade until checked in value (although not in volume) by the depression of the 1930s, whereas East and Central Africa's trade came with more of a rush during the 1920s and 1930s, when an excess of imports over exports suggests greater inward investment into these regions than into West Africa. For all the growth of trade, however, its scale remained modest. In the period 1935–39, external trade was worth only some £2 per head of population in West and East Africa. Whatever the notional figure for Gross National Product might have been, foreign trade must still have involved only a small fraction of the total output of these regions. Central Africa's foreign trade was three times as great, at over £6 per capita, making it the most externally oriented and trade-dependent of the three regions.

After the long build-up from the turn of the century to the Second World War, the colonial period closed with the great expansion of commerce which occurred from the late 1940s onwards, propelled by the post-war and Korean War commodity booms. Although measurement in current prices in Table I overstates the change – volume growth was somewhat less dramatic – this was a period when the increase in African export production was particularly substantial [5: *176–80*]. All three regions of Tropical Africa shared in the growth, so that by 1955–59 total per capita trade had risen to approximately £11 in West and East Africa and £38 in Central Africa. The weight of foreign trade in GNP may have doubled over the 1935–39 figure.

Britain's share of African trade is shown in Table II. It varied by region and over time. In the 1890s, over half of West Africa's exports went to, and nearly three-quarters of its imports came from, Britain – a very close commercial relationship which lasted until after the First World War. Between the wars, however, there was a decline in the importance of Britain to West Africa. Central Africa began the colonial period with a very high degree of reliance on Britain for its mainly mineral exports but a lesser reliance on British imports, given a nearby source of supply in South Africa, but here too the tendency was for trade with Britain to decline as a proportion of the total. Conversely, East Africa came under colonial rule with its foreign trade oriented towards India, Egypt and other countries around the Indian Ocean, and here the trend, until 1929 at least, was for an increase in the commerce between metropolis and colony. This was not enough, however, to offset the decline in Britain's share with the

Table II   British Tropical Africa: Trade with Britain as a Percentage of Total Trade (Five-year averages)

	West		East[a]		Central	
	Exports	Imports	Exports	Imports	Exports	Imports
1890–94	50.9	70.7	–	–	–	–
1895–99	50.9	75.3	7.1	11.0	n.a.	n.a.
1900–04	44.1	70.5	9.5	14.3	n.a.	n.a.
1905–09	47.3	70.9	11.2	28.7	90.2	48.4
1910–14	50.5	64.8	25.7	23.5	83.0	54.2
1915–19	70.6	77.1	29.1	22.2	64.7	47.0
1920–24	61.4	70.3	35.4	29.8	51.1	49.4
1925–29	38.9	59.4	45.5	37.2	72.4	47.5
1930–34	34.5	62.2	36.1	33.6	46.6	44.6
1935–39	44.1	46.7	32.2	34.1	49.3	44.9
1940–44	96.4	56.0	38.1	18.1	72.2	29.8
1945–49	66.1	67.1	42.8	35.6	56.4	34.8
1950–54	62.1	50.3	46.0	41.4	58.7	39.0
1955–59	43.9	43.4	25.6	37.4	53.2	37.0

[a] Excludes Tanganyika before 1920.

Sources: As for Table I.

other regions. Between 1905–9 and 1935–39, the trade of British Tropical Africa roughly doubled in value, but Britain's share of that trade had fallen from 52 to 41 per cent. Given the comparatively low values of the trade, Tropical Africa remained marginal as a market for British industry and as a source of supply of raw materials and foodstuffs.

These trends were briefly reversed during and immediately after the Second World War, when Britain's short flirtation with imperial mercantilism once again raised its share in the trade of its African colonies. By 1950–54 the figure was back to 51 per cent, which represented an increased share of a much more rapidly growing commerce.

For a brief span, perhaps, Tropical Africa had some importance for the British economy, offsetting changes in Britain's trade with other parts of the world, such as India. By 1950–54, the value of Britain's trade with Tropical Africa was some 50 per cent greater than its trade with India and Pakistan, and on a per capita basis the difference was even more striking – £6.22 per head in Tropical Africa against £0.82 per head in the Indian sub-continent. There would appear to be, therefore, a certain irony in the fact that British governments were preparing to decolonise at a time when trade with Tropical Africa was becoming more rather than less important to the British economy.

Liberal scholarship largely regards the growth of foreign trade as a central and progressive force in modern African economic history. Trade is seen as an 'engine for growth' or as a 'leading sector', with dynamic and transformative influences on the whole economy [64]. Such linkages between trade and production will be considered at a later point. Conversely, however, those within the dependency school portray the commercial relationship between developed and less developed parts of the world as being unequal and exploitative. One version is the argument that, because of differential wage levels in the two countries, productivity changes in the less developed are passed on through trade to the more developed, in the form of cheaper exports [54]. However, the idea that terms of trade invariably deteriorate against primary producers is wrong. Such research as has been conducted on the terms of trade of British Tropical Africa, mainly on West Africa, reveals a pattern of shifts in relative advantage through time. From 1900 to 1913, terms of trade moved in favour of the African economies. They then deteriorated, as a consequence of the First World War, until approximately 1922. A recovery up to 1929 was terminated by the depression and the Second World War, but from 1945 came the pronounced improvement in terms of trade which encouraged the great post-war export boom [4: 180–5]. Given the logical and empirical weaknesses in the concept of unequal exchange, other writers in the dependency tradition have stressed not trade per se, but rather the way that trade was organised. They see an 'expropriation of surplus' from Africa as a result of the repatriation of so-called 'super-profits' accruing to private capital invested in African trade and production [6: 162–222].

For most of the Colonial period, British metropolitan governments regarded Tropical Africa as a field lying open to private investment rather than as a location for any significant public investment. Admittedly, there was some recognition that one might need the support of the other. Joseph Chamberlain, Colonial Secretary from 1895 to 1903, who was associated with the Birmingham and Midlands metals, engineering and chemical groups of industries,

23

promoted the idea of 'constructive imperialism' in which it was the duty of the state to transform those economically-backward colonies which could not develop without imperial assistance. Large-scale public investment in transport and communications, especially railways, research in tropical medicine and the provision of technical services would create conditions conducive to the attraction of private capital into African and other dependencies [38; 40; 47]. However, a combination of Treasury parsimony, lingering liberal traditions of laissez-faire and an easing of the competitive pressures on the Midlands' industries by other means, prevented such ideals from becoming an immediate reality.

The orthodox view of policy, that the open economy should be inexpensive to manage and that colonial governments should develop an infrastructure from local revenues, crumbled only slowly. It first began to do so, perhaps, in the 1920s, when low-interest Treasury loans of £19 million for irrigation in the Sudan, and a further £13.5 million for railway construction in East Africa, led to the first Colonial Development Act of 1929 [43; 88: 115–38]. These measures were supported as much by Lancashire cotton interests as by Birmingham engineering ones. The Lancashire lobby, having established the British Cotton Growing Association in 1902 to promote cotton cultivation in the Empire, then lost interest in Africa until after the First World War, when doubts about availability and price of American and Indian cotton supplies emerged once again. The origins of 'colonial development' lay rather more in the structural problems of Britain's staple industries than in the supposed 'conversion of the official mind' between 1932 and 1939 [41: 41], although the shock of the depression both in Britain and in the colonies undoubtedly spurred the introduction of the more effective Colonial Development and Welfare Acts of 1940 and 1945.

Frankel's researches (Table III) reveal that up to 1936 public investment in British Tropical Africa, including borrowing by colonial governments from the London capital markets as well as Treasury loans or grants, amounted to a cumulative total of £201.8 million. East Africa obtained the lion's share, but on a per capita basis, the truer measure of significance, Central Africa was the more favoured region. Unfortunately, comprehensive statistics for public investment after 1936 do not exist, but some indication of its likely growth during the terminal stages of colonial rule is the fact that Treasury loans and grants, which for the whole of the 1930s

Table III British Investment in Tropical Africa

	1870–1936: Public		1870–1936: Private		1962: Private	
	Total (£ million)	Per capita (£)	Total (£ million)	Per capita (£)	Total (£ million)	Per capita (£)
West	50.9	2.0	65.8	2.6	192.2	4.2
East	101.9[a]	5.6[a]	42.5[a]	2.3[a]	54.6[b]	2.3[b]
Central	49.0	11.9	64.7	15.7	125.6	14.7
Total	201.8	4.8	172.9	3.6	372.4	4.8

[a] Includes German investment in Tanganyika.
[b] Excludes Sudan.

Sources: S. H. Frankel, *Capital Investment in Africa* (1938), pp. 158–9; D. K. Fieldhouse, 'The Economic Exploration of Africa', in P. Gifford and W. R. Louis (eds), *France and Britain in Africa* (1971), p. 658.

amounted to no more than £4.3 million, rose to £110 million during 1954–58. East Africa once again received more than the other two regions combined [43: *490–1; 5: 180–1*].

If the role of public investment was to 'prime the pump' for private capital, as Chamberlain had envisaged, it was not particularly successful. Private British investment in Tropical Africa never matched, far less surpassed, the relatively modest amounts of public investment. The £172.9 million which Frankel estimated had been placed in Tropical Africa between 1870 and 1936 (Table III) represented only 58 per cent of the private capital which had been invested in South Africa. Moreover, the method of calculation (adding nominal rather than paid-up capital and making no allowance for company failure) exaggerates the real inflow of private funds into Africa and overstates its importance relative to public investment. By 1962, British corporate investment in Tropical Africa had risen to £372.4 million. Differences in methods of calculation do not permit accurate comparison between the 1936 and 1962 figures – but the idea that, once allowance is made for changes in money values, there was a substantial disinvestment from British Tropical Africa between 1936 and 1962 [36: *633*], seems less than certain. It is more likely that in real terms inward private investment had kept pace with population growth, even if it still lagged behind the increase in public investment, so that by 1962 it was greater than in South Africa and was as much as 15 per cent of British corporate investment in the sterling area as a whole.

Just as Central Africa's foreign trade per capita was greater than that of the other regions, so too was inward private investment more significant for its economic history. The growth of expatriate mining activities, with their heavy requirements for fixed capital, principally for the extraction of gold in Southern Rhodesia and copper in Northern Rhodesia, together with the need for railways to service and support the mining areas, generated a proportionately greater inflow of private investment into the region. In Southern Rhodesia, where gold and other mineral deposits were relatively scattered, mining normally involved small-to-medium corporate enterprises, but the rise of copper-mining in Northern Rhodesia between the wars was conducted by two large mining groups of which one, Selection Trust Ltd, was controlled by American capital and the other, the Anglo-American Corporation, was South African-owned and -based [57].

Although some mining also occurred in West Africa, notably for tin in Nigeria, gold in the Gold Coast and diamonds in Sierra Leone, the typical expatriate business firm there, and in East Africa as well, was the trading house which, with the assistance of banks and shipping companies, handled import-export functions and had less need for fixed capital than an enterprise engaged in primary or secondary production. The British firms in West Africa were in the main descendants of Liverpool houses present on the coast since the arrival of the steamship, if not before. The companies in East Africa were relative newcomers, moving into the region's commodity trades from India, Burma, South Africa and Australia as shipping facilities were developed by the British India and Union-Castle lines [58: *37–47*; 77: *179–290*].

Considerably more controversy surrounds the activities of British mercantile capital in West Africa than in East or Central Africa – possibly because it constituted an older stratum, consolidating its linkages with and influence over other sectors of the economy, whereas in East and Central Africa it was a comparatively new element, discovering a niche and creating linkages virtually from scratch. Thus, the disagreements between contemporaries and historians over the West African shipping conference, whether it should be seen as a monopolistic restraint on, or a force for stability in, West African trade and production [60; 52], had few echoes in East and Central Africa, although these regions were subject to the agreements of South African and Indian shipping conferences. The history of the West African trading firms, it would appear, oscillated between competition and various forms of monopoly. Tendencies towards price-fixing pools and amalgamations in the difficult commercial conditions of the 1880s and 1890s gave way to a competitive phase lasting until approximately 1920. This era was principally characterised by the penetration of the hinterland by the commercial houses, employing railways and river steamers [70]. They established subsidiary posts up-country which were run by their own employees, by-passing and withdrawing credit from local African middlemen on whom they formerly depended [71]. Then, in the 1920s and 1930s, came a new wave of mergers, culminating in the creation of the United Africa Company in 1929 [72], and a return to the use of pooling arrangements in the purchase of agricultural commodities, provoking the Gold Coast cocoa hold-ups of 1930–31 and 1937 [65; 67; 73].

The oligopoly, leaning towards monopoly, of the British mercantile

27

houses, and the almost continual disputes between them, or with local traders, seems to distinguish West Africa from East or Central Africa. In the latter regions, hardly any preliminary build-up of coastal bases or chains of credit to local middlemen preceded the intrusion of British mercantile capital. Apart from such early scouting parties as Smith Mackenzie at Zanzibar, the main body arrived with the railways and established itself up-country almost immediately. It was accompanied by a wave of immigrant entrepreneurs – Indian, South African, Greek, Lebanese and Portuguese merchants and traders – who developed the lower reaches of the commercial hierarchy. Between the 1890s and the 1930s, the lines of commercial competition and alliance in East and Central Africa were more fluid than in West Africa, and the power of the bigger mercantile houses was counter-balanced in some measure by that of immigrant producers' organisations. Consequently, although the details have been too little studied, it would appear that mercantile oligopoly and collusion was confined to certain specific situations, notably in cotton-ginning and exporting in Uganda [88: *237–65*; 90: *436–55*].

The only other significant area of expatriate corporate (as distinct from settler) investment was to be found in plantation agriculture. But for British plantation financiers, conditions in Tropical Africa were much less attractive than those in Tropical Asia [68; 69], so that it was only between the wars, when changing political circumstances in South Asia resulted in a strategy of risk-spreading by plantation firms, that corporate activity made much headway in Tropical Africa – notably in the cultivation of tea and sisal in the East [77: *243–71*; 78: *78–92*].

Did the expatriate businesses exploit Tropical Africa? Neither the relatively privileged position which such firms enjoyed within the colonial economies, nor the fact that their needs and interests usually received fairly close attention from the colonial administrations, nor their advantages of access to finance, technology and managerial expertise, are in dispute. What is less certain, however, is how to evaluate their impact upon the structures of the African economies – did they obstruct and constrain as much or more than they opened up opportunities for economic innovation and growth? Equally controversial is the idea that they impoverished Africa by withdrawing more in the way of profit than they invested or reinvested. Such allegations are usually accompanied by allusions to the profitability of firms which successfully lasted through to the late colonial period, without reference to the evidence of business failure which occurred, more especially before the Second World War [68; 69; 204]. If such losses are taken into account, the average rate of return on British capital invested in Africa may not have been particularly high, a suggestion which seems to be supported by the obvious reluctance of capital to locate itself there. But even in the case of the successful mining, trading, shipping and plantation firms, evidence of 'super-profits' is hard to find because of the relative absence of properly researched business histories. One careful examination of such little evidence as exists concludes that

> Consistently high returns, it seems, accrued to a few firms which managed, with government support, to secure monpsonistic control over local resources and a degree of monopsonistic control over sales by co-operating with other large producers. Evidence of spectacular profits for the few, combined with 'normal' profits for the many (given that higher returns in the colonies were related to higher risks) suggests that the distribution of returns to capital in the colonial era was much the same as in earlier phases of overseas trade with Africa, and, possibly, in frontier trading generally.
>
> [58: *287–8*]

4 The State and the Economy

THE colonial state had a central role in the economic transformation of Tropical Africa, interpreting the broad policy guidelines set out by metropolitan governments and applying them to specific social and ecological conditions. As agents of the metropolitan state, the colonial administrations were expected to operate within the framework of official perceptions about the needs and interests of the British and 'imperial' economies, and at the very least to refrain from actions which might run counter to them. But the free trade and laissez-faire traditions of successive British governments, together with a relatively decentralised system of rule from London which gave wide powers to the governors, meant that colonial authorities had considerable latitude in formulating economic policy. The colonial state itself need not be, and frequently was not, wholeheartedly laissez-faire. With the rise of metropolitan interest in 'colonial development' and Britain's late outburst of mercantilism between the mid-1930s and the early 1950s, the autonomy of colonial government was eroded somewhat, and even occasionally by-passed altogether, but by this time the structural foundations of the colonial economies had already been laid.

Colonial governments certainly recognised that they were expected to assist and promote the growth of external trade and inward investment, but to regard them as mere tools of metropolitan capital, as is the tendency among members of the 'dependency school', is to misunderstand their role. When Lord Lugard, a leading theorist of colonial rule, wrote of a 'dual mandate', balancing the desirability of integrating Tropical Africa more fully into the world economy against the need to protect African societies against possible abuses and excesses of such a process [42], he expressed a concept of the state as arbiter, acting on behalf of the social order as a whole by mediating between different and often conflicting economic interests and social strata. For historians employing Marxist theory, the state served to 'articulate' the different 'modes of production' which co-existed within the territorial boundaries [103; 85]. For all that they were imposed from outside, the colonial governments did not have a free hand to dictate metropolitan or expatriate demands. Their ability to undertake practical functions rested upon some degree of tacit recognition of legitimacy by elements within the African communities. The need to secure and maintain such collaboration placed political constraints upon colonial administrations [46]. This could easily impart a 'conservative' bias to economic and social policies, with the creation of systems of indirect rule taking precedence over, and indeed questioning the desirability of, the promotion of economic and social change in the rural areas [108].

Equally constraining was the basic poverty of the societies they administered. Low per capita incomes, especially monetary incomes, meant that, whether taxes were raised by direct or indirect methods, the state could raise only comparatively small revenues. Such difficulties were compounded by the slow introduction of a progressive income tax, in the face of expatriate or settler groups who were most likely to be affected, and by the fact that, until late in the colonial period, most of the expatriate businesses paid their taxes elsewhere, mainly in London. Attempts to raise the tax levels on African populations could easily lead to social unrest – as in the tax riots in South-East Nigeria in 1929 – and undermine the tacit collaboration of the African political leadership [100: 25–9; 93: 106–17]. Consequently, growth in government finance came about largely through the growth in foreign trade, while trade depression in the early 1920s and most of the 1930s equally meant contraction and/or stagnation in state revenues.

Overall, the state's share of Gross Domestic Product was probably fairly small – the estimate of 5.9 per cent in the case of the Gold Coast in 1930 [115] is perhaps representative for much of Tropical Africa, although the figure may have been higher in Kenya and Southern Rhodesia. Given limited resources, and the fact that expenditures were allocated largely to the agencies of control – the bureaucracy, military, police and judiciary – the ability of the colonial state to transform the local economy was severely circumscribed before 1945. Little wonder, therefore, that it has been depicted as palying a 'night watchman' or 'caretaker' role. Such a description, however, would not be entirely justified. It undervalues even such limited infrastructure of a modern economy as the governments were able to develop, and it tends to ignore the use of powers of control (as distinct from consumption) in the shaping of local economic structures.

Transport innovation, involving harbour improvement, railway construction and a little road-building, was the main, indeed almost the only, state contribution to the formation of social overhead capital. The principal railway lines were constructed up to and including the First World War, with branch and spur lines added during the 1920s. The largest maritime project was the new Takoradi harbour in the western Gold Coast, constructed in the 1920s as part of Governor Guggisberg's ten-year development plan [48]. So slender were the state's resources, however, that the development of basic infrastructure was always a financial gamble. When trade turned down in the 1930s, several administrations discovered, none more acutely than that of Nyasaland [207], that the servicing of debts incurred for transport investment could become a severe burden on public finance. Because of pressures for inexpensive methods of construction and management, levels of operational efficiency were not particularly high [93: *141*] and railway densities in Tropical Africa remained among the lowest in the world. The backward linkages were to British metal and engineering industries. Railways were no 'leading sector' in colonial Africa. Nevertheless, they probably contributed more than any other single factor to the growth of Africa's external and internal trade, and to such economic growth as occurred. The forward effects of a dramatic reduction in transport costs, in a part of the world renowned for its former inefficient and high-cost methods of overland transport, were important in a number of defined locations. The shift of African cultivators into export cash-cropping frequently came hard on the heels of the railway, while for mining centres the importing of heavy engineering equipment, and to a lesser extent the exporting of bulky ores or metals, via the railway was almost a prerequisite for large-scale corporate activity. Claims that certain colonial governments unduly favoured expatriate mining over indigenous agriculture and commerce in the allocation of transport investment and choice of routes [100: *20–1*; 96: *165–76*] are perhaps less than securely founded. What cannot be challenged is the bias shown by the governments of Southern and Northern Rhodesia, as well as Kenya, in allocating land alongside railways to European settler farmers, ranchers and planters rather than to African cultivators.

Land policy was one of the more important economic tools at the disposal of the early colonial administrations. Given relatively low population densities and abundant land, the possibility existed that the colonial state might acquire, or otherwise make available, 'unused' land for the introduction of new forms of agricultural organisation. The principal candidates were the plantation for the mono-cultural cultivation of tropical crops, especially tree-crops, and the grain and/or livestock farm typical of European colonisation in temperate lands. In West Africa, however, there was an unwillingness or inability to proceed too far with a redefinition of African land tenures, particularly as they applied to communal waste or uncultivated land – opposition to such a possibility was particularly fierce in the Gold Coast, where chiefs and their lawyers wanted to keep the alienation of land under their immediate control [226] – and a belief existed among some officials and trading houses that expatriate-owned plantations would undermine African agricultural growth. Consequently, land tended to be made available on terms which did not attract the metropolitan or local expatriate investor. The weight of demand for land for European-owned agricultural enterprises fell mainly on Central and East Africa where, partly as a consequence of initially lower levels of African agricultural commercialisation than in West Africa, colonial governments were more compliant. In Southern Rhodesia and Kenya in particular, administrators took an early decision to encourage and promote the settlement of white farmers from South Africa and Britain. How the land came to be divided into distinctive European and African areas, with legal definition of land rights becoming increasingly based upon racial origins, is of course a central theme in the historiography of these territories [125; 118; 123; 94; 170]. But Northern Rhodesia, Nyasaland, Tanganyika and Uganda also had their pockets of settler-farming communities or proprietary/corporate plantations.

In East Africa, including Kenya, there emerged the idea of a 'dual policy', echoing the concept of a 'dual mandate', in which a European-managed agricultural sector and an African sector would coexist, each producing for international and domestic markets and receiving assistance to do so from the state [119]. However, some historians, adopting the view that European and African agricultural systems were essentially competitive and even incompatible, have questioned the sincerity or practicability of such 'dual policies'. For example, in seeking to explain why European plantations failed to survive on any scale in Uganda after the First World War, discussion has come to revolve around whether the plantations were squeezed out by the greater success of African cash-cropping or failed because of their own marginality in world and metropolitan markets [122; 127; 128]. The largest issue within the debate about the compatibility of European and African agriculture – whether the growth of settler farming in Southern Rhodesia and Kenya stifled the commercialisation of African agriculture in the reserves – will be considered later.

Labour was the principal point of friction between expatriate and settler agriculture and mining on the one hand, and the African communities on the other. Tropical Africa, with its low population densities, had long been characterised by a scarcity of labour for anything other than family-organised enterprises, so that such large-scale units of production and distribution as arose in pre-colonial times tended to do so by the use of servile labour. Opposition to slavery, however, was a central tenet in the capitalist ideology which the British brought with them to Africa, and in accordance with which the new administrations felt obliged to act almost immediately. The means by which the slave minorities in British Tropical Africa were released from ties of personal bondage, and the consequences for local labour markets, have been little studied, but one account of the three-way interplay between the colonial state, Arab landlords and freed slaves in Zanzibar and coastal Kenya [140] highlights the desire of ex-slaves to enter small-holder agriculture rather than become a rural proletariat. The result in Zanzibar, where the continuity of clove-planting was ensured by the transformation of slaves into a tenantry paying a labour rent, is probably untypical. In most of the rest of Tropical Africa, it would appear that former servile labourers moved into small-holder farming on their own account or found employment within the growing transport sector.

However much 'free' labour was created by the end of slavery, it was insufficient to meet the growth of demand for labour for public services, including railway construction, and the new private enter-prises [209; 215; 216]. Employers failed to provide the wages and conditions which would attract the labour of people whose needs for subsistence, and even monetary incomes, could be met from family land. They were either unable to do so, given that prices in world markets were determined by capital-intensive methods employed in the developed economies or by low-wage Indian and Chinese labour in various tropical countries, or they were unwilling to do so, given the prevailing belief in a backward-sloping labour supply curve (meaning that higher wages would produce a faster turnover of labour rather than an increased supply) [214]. One solution might have been to import labour from more densely populated countries, as happened in colonial Southeast Asia, but this was attempted only in the case of Indian labour brought in to build the Kenya railway in the 1890s and promptly repatriated on its completion. The favoured solution was to rely on non-market methods, on the command powers of the state, to create a labour supply. Where public investment and inward private investment were proportionately greatest (Table III), so were demands for state intervention and assistance. While administrative coercion of labour was not unknown in West Africa – for example, in the case of men from the Northern Territories of the Gold Coast recruited for the gold mines by chiefs and officials, or those in Northern Nigeria similarly recruited for railway construction [219; 213] – state intervention in the labour market was most widespread and sustained in East and Central Africa, more especially in Kenya and Southern Rhodesia. Official recruitment of labour for public works (and occasionally for private employers); the raising of levels of direct taxation as demand for labour grew; the cutting back of areas of land reserved for African farming; the introduction of pass controls and legislation to enforce contracts between 'masters and servants': these were among the variety of means by which the colonial state in Kenya and Southern Rhodesia attempted to increase the labour supply between the 1890s and the 1920s [211: *20–147*; 129; 221: *74–127*].

It would be wrong, however, to see the rise of a wage-labour force in Tropical Africa simply in terms of unwilling men and women coerced into employment by the colonial state. Its growth involved a complex interaction between various 'push' and 'pull' factors of which government labour policies were but one – and over time an increasingly less significant one.

While colonial governments in Tropical Africa up to the 1930s developed such rudimentary infrastructure and public services as they could, and adopted land and labour policies to assist the penetration of settler and metropolitan capital, more especially in East and Central Africa, they were unwilling to become too closely involved with production. The frontiers of state intervention stopped well short of the ownership and management of agricultural, mining or manufacturing enterprises. Apart from such odd examples as coal-mines at Enugu in Nigeria, the only state enterprise of any note was the large irrigation scheme in the Gezira area of the Sudan, where the government, in partnership with private capital, organised the cultivation of long-staple cotton for Lancashire's mills [145]. This scheme, matching in scale and vision the irrigation projects of British India, arose out of a combination of relatively unusual circumstances and seems to have had little or no impact upon policy elsewhere in Tropical Africa.

The depression and the Second World War resulted in an increased level of government intervention in the economy [4: *254–66*; 5: *150–74*]. The decline in trade values, shift in terms of trade, fall in public revenues, conflicts between economic interest groups and social unrest which occurred in the 1930s undermined official confidence in the free trade and laissez-faire economy at a time when the metropolitan state was abandoning the old policy prescriptions for the British economy itself. The war-time regulation of Africa's trade and production in the interest of Britain's military and strategic goals gave colonial administrators a taste for, and some experience of, a more sophisticated economic management than previously practised. The liberal economic ideals which, tinged by the authoritarianism of colonial government, suffused policy in most of Tropical Africa up to the 1930s gave way to 'social democratic' ideals of a state-managed mixed economy which were even more palatable to colonial bureaucracies.

Regulation of commodity marketing, one of the principal planks in the 'new colonialism', was partially rooted in the pre-war years when colonial governments had been called upon, or had taken it upon themselves, to settle disputes between producers, middlemen and exporters in the principal staple trades. The depressed conditions of the 1930s imparted much vigour to such disputes. Controls over trade and marketing at its lower levels, at the point of contact between producer and broker or consumer and retailer, came especially early in East Africa, where the dominance of middlemen activities by immigrant Asian traders added a further complication to the politics of commerce [59; 75; 130: *204–13*]. Monopsonistic control boards for export commodities were first pioneered in Southern Rhodesia and Kenya, as props to settler-farming, but their adoption in most of the rest of Tropical Africa came only with the Second World War, when arrangements for the British government to bulk-purchase colonial products suggested the need for state marketing boards in Africa. Most of the great marketing boards which handled Tropical Africa's exports in the post-war years, therefore, were descended from mercantilist institutions and redesigned for changed post-war policy goals. The boards were initially justified as a means of ensuring price stability for producers, it being apparently overlooked that stabilisation of prices could result in the destabilisation of producers' incomes. There was also some confusion of purpose between controlling prices and raising revenue for the state, and in time the marketing boards tended to become fiscal mechanisms, building up sizeable surpluses as a result of the rapid growth of export earnings and releasing part of their funds to general expenditure on 'development and welfare'.

The marketing boards have attracted hostile historical assessment. The nationalist perspective, shared by dependency writers, tends to depict them as the cornerstone of a post-war programme to exploit the African farmer, by denying him the world market price for his commodity, and to prop up the value of the pound sterling by transferring to London the sizeable reserves accumulated by the boards [87: *170–7*]. This is certainly what happened – the reserves of the African marketing and currency boards held in London amounted to £720 million at the 1956 peak – but it is far from clear that this was the intention behind the creation of the institutions. Some liberal critics, on the other hand, see the marketing boards, and indeed all administrative regulation of trade, as evidence of a colonial paternalism which was essentially 'anti-capitalist' and 'anti-developmental' – by blunting the edge of the market, it stifled the development of commercial skills and entrepreneurial spirit among African traders and peasants, as well as obstructing 'the spread of cash-crops, the accumulation of private capital, and the development of prosperous peasantry and of an independent middle class' [89; 34: *649*; 50]. Such views, expressing faith in Adam Smith's 'invisible hand', imply that a continued reliance on free trade and laissez-faire would have been the better policy for the late colonial period. As a counter-factual hypothesis, this appears incapable of either proof or disproof.

The powers of the state were considerably expanded in the post-war years. Access to the surpluses of the commodity marketing boards and the introduction of more sophisticated fiscal measures, including income and corporate taxes, brought about a significant increase in the state's share of GDP. By 1958 in East Africa, for example, it had risen to approximately 15 per cent of GDP in Uganda and Tanganyika and 19.3 per cent in Kenya. Financial assistance from London, in the shape of loans and grants from the Colonial Development and Welfare Fund, were perhaps less important than metropolitan publicity suggested – as critics of late colonial policy point out, the sums coming in were surpassed by the marketing and currency board surpluses going out to be banked in London. Moreover, few of the colonial governments relied upon straightforward grants to finance their post-war development plans. Most public investment still came from locally generated revenues. What distinguished the late colonial period was the greater scale of such investment as a consequence of brisk, export-led economic growth and the state's larger share of domestic product.

Space prevents any substantial discussion of the development plans of the late colonial period, which co-ordinated the enlarged expenditures of government departments and agencies [45]. Although priorities varied from territory to territory, the emphasis was still on the improvement of economic infrastructure. Road construction took over from railways as the focal point of investment in transport, harbours were modernised and enlarged, and electrification was promoted (most dramatically through the Owen Falls dam in Uganda, the Kariba dam between Southern and Northern Rhodesia, and the planning for the Volta River project in the Gold Coast). Urban facilities, such as sanitation and water supply, received attention, and larger sums were now allocated to education and health. Official opposition to industrialisation disappeared, and there emerged, in the shape of the development corporation, the first institution designed for state promotion of manufacturing industry [4: 279–84; 5: 183–5; 93: 225–92]. The colonial administrations seemed to have finally abandoned 'caretaking' in favour of 'building'.

But 'building' to what end? Claims that the purpose of 'colonial development' was to improve the prospects for British industry and British industrial capital within the post-war international economy [78: 99–135; 130: 126–33] deserve both recognition and respect. More efficient production of export commodities, faster economic growth and higher per capita incomes in colonial Africa were likely to lead to an increase in demand for British manufactures and even create conditions conducive to industrial investment in Tropical Africa. Such indeed were among the results of post-war economic planning, at least up to the mid-1950s. However, one may be confusing consequence with intention, and placing too great an emphasis on the attraction of inward private investment within the strategies of the

38

colonial governments. The latter have been subject to too little research by historians for any balanced perspective to emerge.

The mushroom-like growth of government departments and quasi-government agencies, the influx from Britain of technical experts who were too frequently ignorant of African conditions [230], and the tendency of late colonial administrations to regulate all aspects of economic activity, would appear to have contributed more to the growth of the state apparatus than of the economy, and 'an overdeveloped state in an underdeveloped economy' may not be an inappropriate description of the condition of colonial Africa in the 1950s. The rise of interventionism in East Africa has been portrayed as a 'second colonial occupation' [106: *12–16*] and the pressures on the African population regarded as the principal source of the popular dissatisfaction behind the rise of nationalism [104]. Whether this is equally true of West Africa, where emergence of nationalism and the state's adoption of a defensive posture came earlier than in the East, or in Central Africa, where the dominance of the Rhodesian settlers and the creation of the Central African Federation gave politics a particular slant, is perhaps open to debate. It would appear to be no accident, however, that the point at which colonial governments attempted to devise and operate new levers of economic management was also broadly the point at which they ceased to be acceptable to African societies.

5 The 'Peasant' Economies

UNDER British rule the activities of many African cultivators became more externally oriented than before. Among Tropical Africa's principal exports (Table IV), the palm oil and kernels, the cocoa and the groundnuts of Nigeria, Sierra Leone and the Gold Coast, the cotton and much of the coffee of Uganda and Tanganyika, and the tobacco of Nyasaland came from African farms which were mostly, although not exclusively, small-holdings worked by family labour. Such territories, where the rise of production for world markets emerged directly out of indigenous agricultural systems and agrarian organisation, may be described as 'peasant economies', for the want of a better generic term, to distinguish them from the 'settler-mining economies' of Southern Rhodesia, Northern Rhodesia and Kenya, where the export sectors were dominated by expatriate and settler-owned mines, farms and plantations. Differences between the two kinds of colonial economy were perhaps less sharply distinctive than the dichotomy suggests. Nevertheless, they are sufficiently embedded in the historical literature to justify a separate consideration of the two groups.

The emergence of African cash-cropping involved both quantitative and qualitative change – the growth of total cultivated acreages, adoption of new crops, allocation of labour to new tasks, and increased commercialisation of the relationships between the household unit of production and the wider society. Such changes were at the heart of what can be described as the making of peasantries. The definition of 'peasants' by historians of Africa is a distinctive one that may not meet with recognition everywhere: 'Peasants can be distinguished from subsistence cultivators by their involvement in the market and their submission to other social classes' to whom they pay rent or taxes [161: *12*]. The movement of an increasing proportion of African agriculturists along the continuum from subsistence cultivation towards fully commercialised or capitalist farming is one of the central themes in African history, bound up in the rise of the market

Table IV *Principal Exports: Selected African Territories*

	1928		1957	
	Principal exports	*As % of total exports*	*Principal exports*	*As % of total exports*
Nigeria	Palm products	48.3	Palm products	25.8
	Cocoa	14.3	Cocoa	21.1
	Tin	13.1	Groundnuts	20.0
	Groundnuts	10.9	Tin	5.7
Gold Coast	Cocoa	82.4	Cocoa	55.9
	Gold	5.0	Gold	10.7
			Manganese	9.8
Sierra Leone	Palm products	71.5	Diamonds	42.8
			Iron Ore	29.1
			Palm products	15.0
Sudan	Cotton	64.1	Cotton	40.2
Tanganyika	Sisal	28.7	Sisal	24.4
	Coffee	19.1	Cotton	16.9
	Cotton	12.8	Coffee	13.8
Kenya	Cotton	37.3	Coffee	41.3
	Coffee	19.3	Coffee	41.3
	Sisal	7.4	Sisal	7.9
Uganda			Coffee	47.1
			Cotton	38.1
S. Rhodesia	Gold	38.6	Copper	51.6
	Tobacco	12.7	Tobacco	18.0
	Asbestos	11.1	Asbestos	5.5
N. Rhodesia	Copper	30.6		
Nyasaland	Tobacco	73.5		
	Tea	10.9		

Sources: *Statistical Abstracts for the British Empire/Commonwealth* (1929, 1957); A. A. Beshai, *Export Performance and Economic Development in Sudan, 1900–67* (1976), pp. 317–18, 336.

and the growth of state formations. The origins of African 'peasantries' pre-dated the colonial period – wherever towns and trade had emerged there were small-holders producing foodstuffs or raw materials for sale or for taxes. The intensity of such activities, however, varied from locality to locality, and by comparison with India, for example, peasantries had yet to be formed in large parts of Tropical Africa at the end of the nineteenth century. Colonial rule, with its amplification of the commercial, fiscal and political pressures on the rural populations, brought about an increase in production for world markets and, to a lesser extent, domestic markets, so that by the 1930s peasantries and 'peasant economies' were typical of much of Tropical Africa.

What is known about the 'cash-crop revolution', as it has been called [182], comes mainly from the research of liberal historians, and the discussion which follows reflects such work. Little attention can be given to the related attempts by Marxist scholars to develop a distinctive framework for African agrarian history based upon concepts of 'pre-capitalist modes of production' and their 'articulation' with capitalism – partly through limitations of space, partly because the achievements appear little more than taxonomy, putting old wine in new bottles [139], and partly because Marxist historians are themselves divided about the utility of the entire approach. In the words of one, 'the single major theoretical impediment to the effective analysis of actual production in the Third World is the concept of a "mode" of production. Reification of this concept (and indeed of "social formation") has been one of the most negative legacies of Althusserian work on Marxist theory' [160: 4–5].

Old myths about conservative and irrational peasants unwilling to change without the benevolent leadership of colonial officials [146], have crumbled in the light of studies which emphasise the innovativeness of African cultivators faced with new market opportunities and which point out how little influence colonial agricultural experts had on decisions as to which crops would bring the best returns in local conditions [147]. The 'vent-for-surplus' model is sometimes invoked to explain the developments of the early colonial period. The model presupposes an area isolated from international markets and which has a surplus capacity for output resulting from underemployed factors of production. Transport improvement, eroding that isolation, makes it possible to bring idle land and labour into production [153; 154; 155]. However, 'vent-for-surplus' has found a less than whole-hearted acceptance. It can appear overly-mechanistic, allowing little or no scope for entrepreneurship, and seems to convey little interest in how the process of responding to changed market conditions actually gets started. In several cases, particularly where it involved adoption of a new or non-food crop – cocoa in western Nigeria, cotton in Uganda or coffee in Tanganyika – elite or minority groups, such as merchant-farmers, chiefs or Christian communities, played crucial innovatory roles in cash-cropping for export [134; 135; 136; 156; 90; 187; 157: *21–3*; 98: *152–6*; 82]. The wider spread of the novel crops, and the 'democratisation' of export production, came after and as a result of demonstration by the pioneers.

More significantly, perhaps, the model's assumptions about the availability of idle, underused resources merely waiting to be brought to bear are less than accurate. Land was certainly abundant, even if it was no free good. Obtaining access to it, particularly for planting tree crops, could necessitate the development of new methods of land purchase [151: *38–160*] or the manipulation of customary laws and practices. Labour, however, was not necessarily an idle resource. Two factors determined the extent to which labour could be regarded as 'underemployed' at the beginning of the colonial period. The first was the extent of prior engagement in production for external or internal markets. Where there had been none or very little – in several parts of East and Central Africa, for example – labour could conceivably be regarded as being 'underemployed' in household subsistence. But where market production already existed, in effect where peasantries had already come into being, the rise of export cash-cropping would seem to have implied a reallocation of labour from former activities as much as, if not more than, the bringing of idle labour into employment. Thus the emergence of cocoa-growing in southern Gold Coast involved some shift of labour time away from production of palm oil and wild rubber [151: *161–77*] while among the Hausa around Kano in Northern Nigeria the first big spurt of groundnut-exporting meant a shift away from supplying foodstuffs to the city [155: *101*]. There were gains to labour, to be sure, but not as great as the 'vent-for-surplus' model might suggest [232].

The second factor was the fact that labour engaged in growing subsistence crops was not necessarily idle all year round – its underemployment could be seasonal in character, with labour fully stretched at planting or harvest periods. Consequently, cash-cropping could only be introduced without disruption of food supplies if it would fit into prevailing farming cycles and techniques. This was less of a problem in the forests and woodlands of the southern parts of West Africa, the East African coast, and the northern shores of Lake Victoria, where cultivation of the principal food crops, mainly plantains and root crops, went on virtually all the year around, but it was a major difficulty for grain-cultivators in the savanna (or grassland) areas which comprised the northern areas of the Gold Coast and Nigeria as well as most of East and Central Africa [182; 144]. The peasantries of the forest zones experienced little difficulty in adopting new crops by comparison with those of the savanna, who faced pronounced dry seasons and irregular rainfall. Grassland areas were therefore the scene of a long-drawn-out, and often inconclusive, struggle between, on the one hand, colonial administrations imposing taxes and wanting to introduce particular crops, and on the other, grain-farmers seeking to resist or avoid the development. The heart of the problem was the ubiquitous activity of the British Cotton Growing Association which, offering supplies of cotton seed and an organisation for marketing the crop, had a strong influence on colonial administrators looking for a viable cash-crop for savanna areas [141]. Cotton was a labour-intensive crop which made heavy demands on family labour time at sensitive points in the seasonal cycle and it was therefore difficult to fit into savanna farming. Nor could it be eaten if harvests were bad or markets depressed. Consequently, savanna peasantries responded to the incentives of cash or pressures of tax by increasing, where possible, the output of existing foodcrops rather than by adopting cotton. The railway built to Kano in the expectation that it would secure cotton supplies for Lancashire proved to be an outlet principally for groundnuts [153; 155]. Similarly, Tiv cultivators in central Nigeria found the sesame (or benniseed) oil-seed a more acceptable export cash-crop than cotton [142]. Yet other communities in the grasslands adopted cotton under some compulsion and protest when alternative methods of income generation were scarce, and they were ready to abandon the crop whenever possible [181; 185]. Cotton became a secure export crop only in the favourable ecological conditions of the northern shores of Lake Victoria and within the closely regulated, irrigated-agriculture of the Gezira scheme. The ability of large numbers of African cultivators to resist or avoid production of a commodity with a high priority in colonial thinking is a measure of the relative independence of the small-holder from the demands and dictates of the state.

The 'vent-for-surplus' model has limited explanatory power. It imposes rigidity on agricultural histories which are better seen as lengthy and flexible adaptations to demographic, ecological, commercial and political conditions, some of which were altered by the arrival of the railway and tax-gathering colonial officials, and others of which were not. The greater ability to produce for overseas markets in the early colonial period was not unimportant – it influenced the allocative decisions of many cultivators and in turn provided the fiscal base for the colonial state – but in agricultural terms the results must be regarded as something less than 'revolutionary'. Only the more favoured localities – those with reliable rainfall and access to rail or water transport – were in a position to take immediate advantage of the international opportunities, but even there the 'new' agriculture came about with only limited changes in farming practices, no technological innovation and a continuing reliance on food-crops grown within the cash-cropping unit of production itself.

Outside such areas, the cultivator's freedom for manoeuvre was even more constrained. While the urban-commercial sector was growing, it was still relatively small-scale, and the export-oriented agricultural districts were largely self-sufficient in staple foods, so that any enlargement of demand for foodstuffs was probably a modest one, and may have been more to the advantage of specialist producers of proteins than the everyday starchy staples. Where a wedge of expatriate mines or plantations intruded into the local economy, opportunities for commercial food-cropping were increased, and nearby agricultural communities – the peasant farmers of western Gold Coast or northeast Tanganyika, for example – preferred to supply food rather than to work in gold mines or sisal plantations. Where no cash-cropping for export or internal markets was possible, in the extensive areas remote from modern transport, little transition from a subsistence to a peasant way of life occurred. Here migratory labour over long distances was usually the only means of access to cash incomes.

At an early point, therefore, the 'peasant economies' developed those regional characteristics – patterns of inequality based upon a threefold spatial division – which persisted throughout the colonial period.

First, there were regions which specialised in production for export
. . . These were surrounded by a second category of regions which
supplied the export producing regions with food and other services
. . . Finally, spreading out beyond the export and food-producing
regions were peripheral regions which either supplied migrant
labour or stagnated in near isolation from the territorial economy.

[157: *30*]

The regional boundaries were loosely defined and, being determined
in the main by transport costs, were liable to change over time.
During the 1920s, in particular, the development of feeder roads to
the railways, the introduction of motor lorries and, in savanna areas,
animal-drawn carts for transportation of crops, the terminal decline
in head porterage and the end of compulsory labour for carriage of
government loads, all resulted in an intensification of activity in
established areas of peasant production, a transformation of previously marginal areas into established ones, and a general encroachment of market-oriented agriculture into the more remote areas [181;
4: *196–7*; 96: *170–1*; 90: *458–9*].

Gains from foreign trade were by no means equally distributed.
Apart from the regional inequalities within colonial territories, or the
inequalities of productivity and price associated with particular
crops, which gave the average West African cocoa-producer a higher
income than the average East African cotton-farmer, the cash-
cropping societies were themselves internally differentiated. There
was always a minority which, acquiring more land and hiring labour
to cultivate it, produced on a larger scale. This upper stratum was
partly 'seigneurial' in character: chiefs who employed patronage and
clientship to secure labour for their own farms, or who lived off the
rents of cash-cropping tenants and in some measure directed their
agricultural activities, obviously differed in social status and economic orientation from the average small-holder. In East Africa, at
least, the development of the 'gentry' element was checked – among
the Ganda of Uganda and the Haya of Tanganyika, for example – by
changes in land legislation during the 1920s which, intended to turn
chiefs into salaried bureaucrats, gave greater security of tenure and
fixity of rent levels to the tenants, and constrained further growth in
estate or 'desmesne' farming [90: *453–5*; 187: *48–55*; 98: *281–3*; 82:
170–3].

The other element, sometimes conflicting with the 'seigneurial' one and sometimes in alliance with it, was 'capitalist' or 'petty bourgeois'. It comprised that minority which combined commercial farming with trading and/or white-collar employment in government service or the professions. The growth of cash-cropping, it is becoming clear, was bound up with the development of opportunities for off-farm earnings. Capitalisation depended as much upon mobilising cash from outside agriculture as from ploughback of profits from cultivation. Some sources of credit were available – the cocoa-farmer in western Nigeria was able to pawn his trees and traders in northern Nigeria were known to offer cultivators advances against the coming season's groundnut crop [136: *102–3*; 155: *86–7, 143–4*] – but on the whole systems of rural credit were not as highly developed as in rural Asia. The successful farmer, therefore, the one able to increase the size of operations and enjoy whatever economies of scale were available to particular crops, usually had other sources of income. Frequently, this meant trading in, or processing, agricultural commodities.

A more commercialised and export-oriented agriculture needed an expansion in marketing and distributive trades – for bulking-up the produce from a large number of small farms and the breaking-down of imported goods into the small quantities retailed to the individual peasant household. In West Africa, this came about through the growth and modification of existing networks for external and internal commerce – the Hausa traders who pioneered groundnut-buying in northern Nigeria, for example, had previously been engaged in the kola trade from Asante to Kano – but in East Africa, and to a lesser extent in Central Africa, marketing and distributive systems were created virtually from scratch by immigrant Asian traders [62; 59]. In Uganda, Tanganyika and Nyasaland, the Indian *dukawallah* (store-keeper) represented the crucial link between the peasantry and the wider economy, although as time went on his role was challenged by African traders diversifying out of agriculture.

The history of petty-commodity trading in colonial Africa still remains to be written. That it too experienced evolution and fluctuation is suggested by occasional glimpses into its operations – by studies, for example, which demonstrate how the penetration of expatriate mercantile houses into Eastern Nigeria undermined the older strata of independent middlemen while creating new opportunities for Africans as company agents [71], or how cocoa-broking in the Gold Coast was initially conducted by men who were also cocoa-farmers but during the 1920s became the function of a mercantile element with no agricultural investments [76]. However, the principal contours of the petty-commodity trades remain too little known to permit broad comparative generalisation about the direction and character of change.

The years from the 1890s to 1929, crucial to the structural development of the 'peasant economies', can be regarded as an 'age of improvement'. Although frontiers of cash-cropping enterprise still lay well short of the territorial boundaries, the growth of incomes from export production seems to have been accomplished at little or no cost to aggregate food supply. It would appear, although no precise quantitative measurement is possible, that agricultural output had grown faster than population and that some meagre improvements in welfare may have been achieved. Between 1930 and 1945, however, no economic growth occurred – there may even have been some decline in per capita output. Peasants, traders and governments were all engaged in attempts to find ways to overcome the stagnation or decline in incomes, profits and revenues, which frequently meant exploiting whatever opportunities existed for production and exchange within the domestic economy as well as the disarticulated world economy [4: *254–67*; 5: *150–74*; 98: *342–75*]. But these were essentially short-term expedients, and the structures of the 'peasant economies' remained frozen in the patterns of the late 1920s.

When the thaw came from the late 1940s onwards, the structures were modified without being substantially altered. The considerable recovery in international commodity prices, renewed public expenditure on road-building and private investment in motor vehicles, and a growing population resulted in further increases in the acreages devoted to export production. The principal export crops of 1957 were still those of 1928 (Table IV), albeit with some minor shifts in their relative importance. More land was brought under cultivation around the margins of cash-cropping areas, while formerly peripheral areas moved into export production for more or less the first time; tobacco-cultivation in the Bunyoro province of Uganda or rubber-growing in the Benin (Mid-West) Province of Nigeria, for example, were among the innovations of the post-war years. Given more rapid rates of urbanisation, promoted by the expenditure patterns under government development plans, the domestic market for agricultural commodities expanded even more rapidly than export markets, and

48

here too there were signs of an increased output in response. African peasantries remained capable of the kinds of initiatives which had occurred before 1930.

But the limitations of peasant agriculture were also beginning to emerge more clearly. The post-war growth of small-holder incomes came about mainly as a consequence of improved commodity prices and an increase in the area under cultivation. Improvements in productivity would appear to have made little significant contribution. The evidence on agricultural productivity (whether per acre or per man) is confused and ambiguous, not just from lack of hard statistical evidence but because colonial agriculture officials of the period were torn between stressing the conservatism of African agricultural methods and emphasising the improving effects of their own efforts. In northern Nigeria, groundnut yields remained constant – a government campaign to promote a higher-yielding variety which needed artificial fertiliser failed because the peasant farmers found the fertilisers too expensive – while in western Nigeria an increase in cocoa yields per acre resulted merely from new plantings, which replaced ageing trees and brought productivity back to the levels of the 1920s [149: *83, 113–18*; 155: *147–8*]. In Uganda, meanwhile, 'the increase in cotton and coffee cultivation can be mainly attributed to a growing population following a broad pattern of farming already laid down' [107: *219*], and 'it is doubtful whether the efficiency of agricultural methods had been much improved' before the end of the colonial period [130: *76*]. Examples of technological innovation by individuals can, of course, be found – as in the spread of ox- and tractor-ploughing in Tanganyika [98: *455–6*] – but how far this raised the overall per capita output in agriculture is less than clear.

Given that the attention of agricultural departments and research institutes focused more on export crops than on staple foodcrops, it seems likely that productivity in the latter lingered even further behind. Since production of foodstuffs, for subsistence and local sales, comprised perhaps as much as 75 per cent of total agricultural output, it would appear that there could have been only a limited increase in agricultural productivity over the colonial period as a whole. Whether this is to be explained by the failures of colonial governments – their alleged lack of understanding of or sympathy for peasant agriculture, and stultification of its operations by bureaucratic regulations and controls [89] – or by the harsh and difficult environment against which Africa's peasantries had to struggle [131], or by the fact that African agriculture was a comparatively late entrant into world commodity production, or by some combination of these or other factors, remains open to discussion and debate.

6 The 'Settler-Mining' Economies

SOUTHERN Rhodesia, Northern Rhodesia and Kenya constitute a distinctive category within Britain's colonial territories – as export economies in which production for world markets was conducted principally by expatriate- and immigrant-owned mining and agricultural enterprises. These three territories attracted the largest European immigration into British Tropical African (Table V), in the

Table V   Immigrant Populations in East and Central Africa
(000's)

	European		Asian	
	1935–6	1956–62	1931	1956–61
S. Rhodesia	55.4	221.5	1.7	7.2
N. Rhodesia	9.9	74.5	0.1	7.8
Nyasaland	1.8	8.7	1.6	10.6
Kenya	17.9	55.7	43.6	176.6
Tanganyika	8.4	20.5	23.4	76.5
Uganda	1.9	10.8	13.0	71.9
Zanzibar	n.a.	0.5	14.2	18.3
Sudan	n.a.	6.8	n.a.	12.8

Source: F. Dotson and L. O. Dotson, 'The Economic Role of Non-indigenous Ethnic Minorities', in L. H. Gann and P. Duignan, *Colonialism in Africa, 1870–1960: Vol. 4, The Economics of Colonialism* (Cambridge, 1975), pp. 612–13.

shape of fragments of Anglo-South African society scattered across Central and East Africa wherever mineral deposits and high ground considered suitable for colonisation could be found. Although outnumbered by the African inhabitants, the settlers enjoyed a considerably greater degree of representation in government (amounting to full internal self-government in Southern Rhodesia from 1923) and secured significant levels of state assistance in attaining their economic and social goals. As owners and managers of capitalist enterprises, they made much greater use of wage labour than did peasant farmers. Consequently, the development of a wage-labour force proceeded further and faster in the three 'settler-mining' economies (Table VI) than elsewhere in Africa (with the exception of Nyasaland, where labour migration into the Rhodesias and South Africa developed out of special circumstances).

Table VI   Wage Employment in British Tropical Africa
(Total wage employment as a percentage of the economically active population)

	1938	1960–63
Nigeria	4.7	5.1
Gold Coast/Ghana	8.3	19.9
Sierra Leone	4.6	6.0
Kenya	26.2	20.5
Tanganyika	16.2	10.1
Uganda	7.9	8.9
S. Rhodesia	33.5	52.0 [1956]
N. Rhodesia	44.1	25.4
Nyasaland	44.1	16.3

Source: C. W. Newbury, 'Historical Aspects of Manpower and Migration', in P. Duignan and L. H. Gann; *Colonialism in Africa: Vol. 4, The Economics of Colonialism* (Cambridge, 1975), p. 532.

The salient features of the early 'settler-mining' economies are perhaps well enough known. Throughout much of East and Central Africa patterns of land occupation and use had been disturbed by the great ecological crises of the late nineteenth century – by the pandemics of rinderpest, smallpox and sleeping sickness which devastated cattle herds and human population [228; 225; 231] – and the pressures on the African populations were added to, particularly in Southern Rhodesia, by the violence attendant upon the colonial intrusion. Initial settler penetration, therefore, came at a low point in the history of many of the African communities. In Southern Rhodesia it soon transpired that there would be no 'Second Rand' – gold and other mineral deposits were too small and scattered to sustain the interest of London and South African finance houses – and gold-mining was therefore 'reconstructed' between 1903 and 1910 to facilitate the entry of smaller, local settler enterprises. Thereafter the intensity of extraction of gold, asbestos and various base metals expanded and contracted in accordance with world prices [203; 221: *11–33*]. Until the mid-1920s, Northern Rhodesia experienced little immigrant activity other than the recruitment of labour for mines in Southern Rhodesia and the Katanga (Shaba) province of the Congo (Zaïre). Thereafter, exploitation of the ores of the Copperbelt by the two big expatriate mining groups created a string of mining townships along the northern border and resulted in Northern Rhodesia becoming the second largest copper-exporting economy in the world. Associated as it was with the growth of the electrical and motor-car industries, the Copperbelt was more central to Britain's industrial needs and interests than any other part of Tropical Africa [193; 83; 189].

Settler farmers came into the two Rhodesias to produce grain and livestock to feed the mining populations, and in the southern territory to develop tobacco cultivation for the British market. Successive divisions of the land into European and African areas, culminating in the Land Apportionment Act of 1930, gave the Europeans of Southern Rhodesia over 60 per cent of the total acreage, most of it in the relatively favoured high-veld [170]. Meanwhile, in the Kenya highlands a smaller European farming community emerged, one which lacked a local mining market for its maize and other foodstuffs and which came to depend mainly upon the cultivation of high-quality *arabica* coffee. Here too, land allocation was highly favourable to the settler community, with approximately 20 per cent of the usable land set aside for its use [125; 130: *33–9*; 118; 123: *47–88*]. Until the Second World War at least, European producers of grains and livestock in East and Central Africa were not particularly efficient by international standards, so that they required a range of state assistance, from special railway freight rates for Kenya's maize farmers to government-subsidised cold-storage facilities for Southern Rhodesia's beef producers [173], to enable them to compete in world markets.

Early assessments of the evolution of the 'settler-mining' economies focused upon the growth of export production and tended to rely upon the concept of a 'dual economy' to explain why the benefits of participation in world trade had appeared to accrue primarily to the European sector. Economic dualism was defined as a situation where

53

a money economy, organised and financed largely by Europeans and heavily dependent upon external trade and investment, grew up alongside the African economies where techniques were relatively backward, productivity was low, and real income barely rose above the minimum required for subsistence. The agrarian way of life practised in the African reserves was seen as a 'traditional economy' or sector, which yielded up surplus labour to the expanding European sector, but otherwise remained little changed over time [84: 4–5; 83: 40–1, 58–9]. However, as historians began to pay more attention to the incorporation of the African communities into the colonial economy, dissatisfaction with the 'dual economy' approach began to grow, and at its extreme, inspired by Marxist scholarship, threw up an entirely contrary model of the 'settler-mining' economy. 'Dualism in Rhodesia (i.e. the technological, economic and political distance between the two races) was less an "original state" . . . than it was the outcome of the development of capitalism itself' [81: 222].

The new model emphasised the role of government in advancing the interests of the European sector and discriminating against the African one, primarily with the intention of providing the former with abundant supplies of cheap labour. The result of state intervention was the long-run impoverishment of the African reserves – as in South Africa, so too north of the Limpopo, 'the structural underdevelopment of the peasant sector was the other side of the coin of capitalist development' [172: 228]. In the early days of the colonisation of Southern Rhodesia, before the full emergence of European farming, it was argued, an African peasantry had come into being, based upon the sale of foodstuffs to centres of mining, transport and commercial demand, but the development of a peasantry ran counter to the needs of the mines and the later-arriving settler farmers for labour from the reserves. Consequently, a whole range of state policies – heavy direct taxation of Africans, occasional forced labour, pass controls, assistance for employers' recruitment organisations, redefinition of reserves to shift Africans on to poorer soils and away from transport facilities, and a neglect of public services in the reserves – created conditions in which European farmers secured the greater part of the market for agricultural commodities and the settler sector as a whole obtained cheap labour from stagnant and impoverished African lands. Although evolving out of the debate within Southern Rhodesian historiography, the new view had wide appeal, so that historians of Kenya, too, began to write about 'the rise and decline of

54

the Kenya peasant' [132] or 'the steady disintegration of the traditional African peasant economy' [123: *144*]. The so-called 'proletarianisation' of African rural societies came to be seen as a process common to all the 'settler-mining' economies:

> Thus by the end of the 1930s, the agricultural economy of the Shona and the Ndebele, like that of the Kikuyu and most South African peoples, had been destroyed. The struggle between 'the European farmer seeking to reduce the African to a proletarian and the African seeking to retain the maximum amount of economic independence' had been won conclusively by the Europeans.
>
> [171: *243*]

How valid and useful is this line of interpretation? Undoubtedly, studies employing the 'dual economy' framework gave too little attention to structural relationships and failed to appreciate the extent to which mobilisation and allocation by the colonial state involved a transfer of resources from the African to the European sector. This operated through fiscal policy, with Africans paying considerably more in taxes than they received in the way of public services [88: *190–9*; 167: *43–4*], through land policy, and above all through labour policy. That African cultivators showed an initial reluctance to undertake wage employment while prospective employers failed to provide the level of wages and conditions which would induce men to enter permanent employment – health and housing conditions in the early Southern Rhodesian mines were particularly poor – and that a range of government measures, including compulsion, was largely instrumental in securing an increase in labour supply up to the early 1920s, has been amply documented in a number of studies [211; 221; 218]. From the early 1920s, however, the migratory labour system which had been brought into existence became more 'voluntary' in character and assumed a volition of its own, as modest improvements in employment conditions, largely a result of government prodding, lessened dislike of wage labour; as the use of residential or 'squatter' labour helped to solve the labour supply problems of European farmers and reduced their demands for state assistance; as some younger Africans discovered in the better paid jobs a means to accumulate savings to start their own household production and reproduction; as yet others found that, with demographic growth, the household land-holding was becoming insufficient to support the entire family; and as large areas, especially in Northern Rhodesia, remained remote from markets and precluded from any other means of obtaining money for taxes, consumer goods or school fees. The motives for participating in migratory labour, the interaction of 'push' and 'pull' factors, became extremely complex, differentiating between rural districts and individuals within these districts [160: *153–4, 241–79*; 218: *80–9*; 210: *12–18*; 171: *339*].

The migratory labour system was a hybrid or compromise solution to the struggle between two sets of needs and interests. On the one hand, inefficient settler enterprises, normally undercapitalised, employing technology which was often not much more advanced than that of the African cultivators but attempting to operate on a larger scale, shackled by high transport costs for imported inputs and consumer goods and exported commodities, and facing world prices set by more efficient producers elsewhere, needed labour simply to survive. On the other hand, African societies contained no rural proletariat, and their agriculture had seasonal fluctuations in levels of employment, as well as divisions of function between sexes and ages, which made it difficult to release 'surplus' labour for any lengthy period. Short-term migratory labour, generating a very high rate of turnover within the workforce, was one means of bridging the gap. Another was the residential or 'squatter' system, used by agricultural estates with abundant land, whereby Africans obtained access to land for cultivation or herding in return for a labour-rent. The system, with its attendant paternalistic relationships between landlord and 'tenant-at-will', was perhaps closer to a 'seigneurial' than a capitalist form of agricultural organisation. Metropolitan or expatriate firms coming in during the 1920s, to mine copper in Northern Rhodesia or plant tea in Kenya, accepted the migratory labour arrangements already in existence. They too had needs for large amounts of unskilled labour and brought with them, from South Africa and India, methods which were compatible with migrant labour, but they were also more sensitive than settler primary producers to the inefficiencies of the system and the advantages of moving away from it.

Some scholars, working within a Marxist framework of analysis, see the relationship between capital and labour in the early 'settler-mining' economies as a process of 'primary capital accumulation' – of a particular type. By contrast with early modern Europe, where according to Marx the powers of the state were used to separate people from the means of production, the state in 'settler-mining' colonies created a 'semi-proletariat', the existence of which was beneficial to employers in that they secured cheap labour. Wage-rates set at levels needed to support a single man threw the costs of maintaining the worker's wife and family on to the reserves: capital obtained labour at less than the cost of reproduction [81: *222–3*; 15: *255–6*; 129: *275–93*]. This should not be taken to imply, however, that settler capitalism was any more 'exploitative' of labour, in the Marxist sense, than any other kind of capitalism, for 'labour-value' theory suggests that the more skilled the labour force the higher the rate of 'exploitation'. The migrant and 'squatter' labour force was unskilled and ill-suited to capital-intensive methods of production and distribution. It resulted from the interaction between a relatively weak capitalism on the one hand and on the other rural societies which remained relatively secure in their ownership of the means of production.

But to focus on 'the way in which state institutions and policies were shaped to serve the settlers', it has been argued in the case of Kenya, is merely to recognise a 'salient half-truth' [103: *493*]. What is at issue is less whether, or even how, labour came to be mobilised for European-owned enterprises, than the effects that mobilisation had on agriculture and agrarian life within the African reserves. In Kenya, the same study asserts 'peasant commodity production, far from being "destroyed", continually expanded despite the imposed dominance of settler production' [103: *494*]. That the development of a cash-cropping peasantry was by no means incompatible with the growth of estate agriculture is a major conclusion of the recent historiography of colonial Kenya [184; 167: *165–88*; 160]. Although the settler estates received a disproportionate amount of state assistance and virtually monopolised export production – Africans were actually prohibited from growing such crops as coffee and pyrethrum – the emergent peasantry undersold them in domestic markets for foodstuffs, above all grain for human and livestock consumption. Although the division between settler maize for export markets and African maize for domestic markets broke down briefly in the 1930s, when very low world prices drove estate products back on to local markets, over the colonial period as a whole African grains, pulses, vegetables and poultry fed the urban populations and plantation workforces. The expansion of cropped acreages within the reserves was made possible in part by social differentiation, which enabled some cultivators to hire, or otherwise secure, labour in competition with the settler estates, but in the main it came from an increase in the work-load of the female members of peasant households whose male members worked for some part of the year in the European sector [160: 55, 93]. Women bore the brunt of the changes in labour allocation.

The 'rise and fall of the peasantry' thesis is inappropriate to Kenya's economic history, and was never seriously argued for Northern Rhodesia where, once mining got under way, the demand for foodstuffs was greater than the output of settler-farms and came to be supplied in part by African peasantries [83: 140–62; 168]. What then of its relevance for Southern Rhodesia, whence it first emerged? The fragmentary quantitative data on African agriculture in Southern Rhodesia points to no long-term decline in per capita grain output, but rather to fluctuation around a static trend [166]. This reveals little about the degree of commercialisation, which has yet to be seriously studied, but sufficient doubts have been thrown on the evidence both for early growth of commodity sales by small-holders and its alleged decline later [175; 163] to suggest that the pattern of events in Southern Rhodesia may not have been too dissimilar from that in Kenya [233].

To rescue the peasantry from the oblivion of the 'traditional economy' or of the 'labour reservoir', however, must not be to adopt too rosy a view of its condition. Such cash-cropping as occurred before the Second World War did so more despite government than with its aid, and it brought lesser monetary rewards than cultivation of export crops. Pressures on African societies were greater in 'settler-mining' economies than in 'peasant' economies and there were many more constraints upon freedom of action – not just the absence of large numbers of the male population for parts of the year but also the strict division of land between the races and the imposition of fixed land boundaries which, with demographic growth, put the rural communities under some stress. As the reserves began to fill up, a land shortage developed in the more densely populated areas and land-extensive agricultural techniques became progressively less appropriate. Shortening of fallow periods, adoption of plough cultivation and livestock accumulation within a situation of growing land scarcity produced some decline in natural fertility and an increase in soil erosion. Agronomic deterioration and land litigation represented the underside of agricultural commercialisation [179: *34–47*; 167: *189–223*; 170: *201–5, 218–22*].

Broadly, the period 1930–45, when depressed commodity prices coincided with growing population pressure on land, was a low point in the fortunes of the African agrarian communities. After the war came some improvement. The state in the late colonial period took upon itself the management of African land which previously it had largely neglected. In Northern Rhodesia it was enabled to do so by the copper boom which, between 1946 and 1957, saw the price of copper triple and output double. Although, after 1953, most of the resultant increase in public revenues accrued to the new Federation of Central Africa, and therefore indirectly to Southern Rhodesia, the administration of Northern Rhodesia was more favourably placed than before to allocate financial resources to the rural areas. The principal changes, however, came in Southern Rhodesia and Kenya. In both territories the Second World War brought benefits to European agriculture. Demand for foodstuffs for the Allied war effort in the Middle East and elsewhere, a certain amount of war-induced industrialisation, and a system of produce control boards with strong settler representation [11: *97–104*; 180], secured profits for European grain and livestock producers which, in turn, helped to finance a post-war shift to more capital-intensive methods. The successful movement towards mechanised grain-farming and intensive dairy-farming, the adoption of high-value virginia tobacco in Southern Rhodesia, and the rising prices in international commodity markets, all served to weaken settler fears of competition from the peasant producer while at the same time reducing their need for unskilled labour. Consequently, governments in Southern Rhodesia and Kenya were able to give more attention to the regeneration and growth of African agriculture.

At first, this meant little more than a revival of the pre-war concern with soil conservation and cattle culling, but by the 1950s administrative action had acquired broader goals. In Kenya in particular, the 'Mau Mau' revolt, which had resulted from earlier failures to deal with the problems of Kikuyu squatters being squeezed out of the 'White Highlands' by the changes in agricultural techniques, transformed official policy. A deliberate programme of 'peasantisation' was adopted, the cornerstone of which was the Swynnerton Plan of 1954 which aimed to consolidate land-holdings and institute individual tenure in the African reserves regarded as having high-to-medium agricultural potential. The reforms in tenure, although never imposed throughout the highlands and perhaps less inegalitarian in practice than officials had first intended, hardened the prevailing patterns of social differentiation within the peasantries, so that those with the larger holdings tended to be the beneficiaries of the second aspect of the programme – state promotion of cash-cropping. The denial of export markets to African cultivators, which had been weakening since the 1930s, was finally abandoned and African cash-cropping became much more diversified. Coffee, pyrethrum, tea, sisal, cotton, tobacco and rice were among the new peasant crops which, together with settler farming, secured a growth of 39.3 per cent in total agricultural output in Kenya between 1954 and 1962 (compared with only 5.3 per cent in neighbouring Uganda) [179; 110; 137; 178; 186; 160: *315–74*].

Events in Southern Rhodesia moved in a roughly parallel direction. The setting aside, in 1950, of an additional nine million acres of land for African occupation was intended to stave-off land hunger among former squatters (although settlement of the land proceeded slowly). Meanwhile, in the Native Purchase Areas, originally created in 1930, an elite of land-buying, labour-hiring African farmers modestly flourished in the more favourable commercial conditions of the 1950s. The Land Husbandry Act of 1951, like the Swynnerton Plan in Kenya, attempted to transform the main reserves into individually registered peasant holdings. The aims of this land reform were ambiguous – whether it was merely to try to slow down the movement of population into the urban areas, or more positively to create a stratum of prosperous cash-croppers, remains open to doubt – and it proved difficult to implement in the already crowded condition of most reserves. The policy ended in the early 1960s, when European farmers turned once again to the home market for their produce. Over 1945–60 as a whole, however, there had been some strengthening of the differentiation within the African rural communities and a broadening of their commercial activities; cotton, rice, tobacco and groundnuts were among the new cash crops [170: *241–6*; 158; 174; 143].

For the peasantries in 'settler-mining' economies the late colonial period was a time of trying to catch up on the levels of income and welfare which had already been achieved by small-holders elsewhere in Tropical Africa. This process went furthest in Kenya (and perhaps, although the evidence is less adequate, in Northern Rhodesia). By giving metropolitan policy-makers and expatriate business interests greater confidence in the performance of African agriculture in these countries it weakened the political influence of the European farming communities and contributed to decolonisation. In Southern Rhodesia, however, where substantial political authority had already been yielded to the European population, the struggle between emergent peasantries and an entrenched settler-farming still had further to run.

7 Crafts, Industry and Employment

THE 'open-economy' model accepted by British policy-makers and businessmen for most of the colonial period assumed that growth and development in Tropical Africa would be achieved through trade with the world in general, and with Britain in particular, in a complementary exchange of primary products against manufactures. Such a relationship would not necessarily preclude the emergence of some modern manufacturing industry in Africa, as had indeed occurred in India before 1914, but any industrialisation would have to come about spontaneously, as a result of market forces exploiting conditions of comparative advantage, and should not be 'artificially' induced by the state. Such a policy, it has been argued by nationalist writers from Hamilton and List to present-day dependency theorists [74] merely served to maintain the gap between the less developed and the more developed economy, and the reliance of one on the other. 'Deindustrialisation', in the form of a decline of handicraft industries, would proceed further and faster than the growth of new factory-based manufacturing and industrial employment.

Pre-colonial Africa, while perhaps lacking the range and sophistication of craft goods to be found in pre-industrial Europe, India or the Far East, produced a variety of items for local consumption by simple handicraft methods. What happened to these artisan trades under colonial rule has been less than adequately investigated. Too often historians have merely assumed their disappearance under competition from imports; lists, and even lengthy descriptions, of pre-colonial handicrafts have been supplied and the reader left to imagine their fate [130: *110–22*]. However, where markets for manufactured goods are expanding, a relative decline in market share is still consistent with an absolute increase in output, and it is therefore by no means certain that any major 'deindustrialisation' occurred in British Tropical Africa [4: *250*]. Several studies, indeed, point to the remarkable longevity of African handicraft methods. Cotton textiles in large parts of Nigeria, for example, resisted import penetration as a result of local transport inefficiencies, consumer tastes and marginal labour costs [196; 197], while in the Gold Coast, salt from the lagoons at the mouth of the Volta River continued to be preferred to imported salt throughout the colonial period [206]. Pottery and dried fish are other 'traditional' products which found consumer preference in local markets. Nor must it be supposed that when some branches of handicraft production declined they did so under the pressure of imports. The end of snuff-making in Southern Rhodesia, which undermined the tobacco markets of the Shangwe people, resulted from the introduction of local factory-manufactured cigarettes [162: *283*].

If the extent of change in the established handicraft trades remains somewhat unclear, even less attention has been devoted, for the colonial period at least, to the emergence of new craft trades in construction, services and small-scale manufacturing which may have helped to offset income and employment effects from any contraction in handicrafts. Particularly in the growth phases of the 1920s and 1950s, and especially in the towns and cities, there emerged a variety of small businesses and self-employed artisan workshops such as joinery and brick-laying, blacksmithing with imported scrap iron, tailoring, shoe-making, or motor vehicle repair and servicing, whose role in the economy, as sources of entrepreneurial experience and capital accumulation, or networks for the acquisition and diffusion of new skills, and whose relationship with the older trades as well as with the newer, expatriate and settler enterprises, represented some of the largest gaps in the economic historiography of Tropical Africa.

Modern manufacturing industry, employing relatively advanced technology, came late to colonial Africa. Before the Second World War, such as there was comprised mainly the processing of primary commodities for export – cotton-ginning, coffee-hulling, tobacco-curing or oil-milling – and to a lesser extent for local markets, as in saw-milling or flour-milling. Otherwise, in most colonial territories only the odd consumer goods factory, a brewery here or a cigarette factory there, had set down roots. After the war, industrial growth was much more pronounced and the share of manufacturing in Gross Domestic Product rose. While this resulted partly from a further increase in commodity-processing operations, in the main it was the consequence of import substitution, either low value to bulk imports which required few sophisticated inputs, like cement for the construc-

63

tion industries, or fairly simple consumer goods, such as textiles, clothing, shoes, soaps and detergents, beer and spirits, and cigarettes for the mass market. Post-war industrialisation was therefore limited in character and extent. By 1960, there was still no production of capital goods, and hardly any of intermediate goods; manufacturing retained a high import content, in the form of machinery and even raw materials, and in most of British Tropical Africa the manufacturing sector still contributed as little as 3–6 per cent of GDP. Only Kenya (9.5 per cent) and Southern Rhodesia (16 per cent) stood out above the rest in degree of industrialisation, and they were also the only producers of intermediate goods [199: *471–5*].

What explains the slow and restricted industrial growth in colonial Africa? Deliberate obstruction by colonial governments or metropolitan policy-makers can be ruled out as a principal factor. While some examples can be found of intervention in response to protests by British manufacturers [88: *266–81*; 43: *495–8*], these took place during the difficult years of the 1930s and were not typical of British policy as a whole. On the other hand, prior to the Second World War, colonial governments were not prepared to become involved in the active promotion of industry by way of subsidy or tariff protection. Infant industries had to be sufficiently robust to withstand the chill winds of import competition. Equally constraining were the low levels of per capita incomes which, together with limited transport facilities, meant poor domestic markets for the potential manufacturer. It can be argued that not until the prosperity engendered by the export boom of the 1950s did effective demand for manufactured goods reach the point where local factory production became possible [4: *278*]. Finally, there is the alleged conservatism of the merchant houses, said to be more acute in the case of the more oligopolistic trading conditions of West Africa than the more competitive conditions in East and Central Africa, which did not wish to see displacement of their own importing activities by local manufacturing and which lacked both the expertise and the incentive to engage in manufacturing investment themselves [199: *490–1*].

Consideration of the exceptional cases of Southern Rhodesia and Kenya, however, throws doubt on some of these propositions. Although Southern Rhodesia's per capita income was probably no greater than the Gold Coast's, or Kenya's than Nigeria's, industrialisation began earlier in these 'settler-mining' economies, that is in the inter-war years. Such manufacturing was undertaken, however, not by the 'more competitive' expatriate trading houses but by the lesser, settler businessmen, British or South African in Southern Rhodesia, British or Indian in Kenya, while governments susceptible to settler influence *were* prepared to provide some modest state assistance to local infant industries [125: *235–6*; 111: *169–79*]. What the immigrant merchant-industrialist supplied, it would seem, was entrepreneurship, combining risk capital with some familiarity with manufacturing processes and technology. Absence of the latter, associated in turn with deficiencies in colonial education policy, especially in respect of technical and commercial education, may be the key to explaining the industrial lag elsewhere.

After the war the immigrant entrepreneurs, like the Chandaria and Madhvani families in East Africa [78: *126–30*], went on to expand and diversify their businesses, but two new elements also became important. First, the colonial state, with its investment in infrastructure and urban services, its development corporation to act as a midwife to new enterprises, its fiscal privileges and its industrial licensing system, adopted a more positive commitment to the promotion of manufacturing. Second, metropolitan industrialists began to invest in Tropical Africa. These two developments were obviously related: the strategy of the late colonial state was to attract inward industrial investment as an alternative to (or substitute for) indigenous or settler capital and entrepreneurship. The metropolitan and international manufacturers often set up in business on their own account, either because of specific invitations from government or fears of being shut out by tariffs, but sometimes too they entered into partnerships with state organisations and private firms, including the expatriate mercantile houses. In West Africa, a notable transformation occurred in the operations of the big trading companies during the mid-1950s. They withdrew from up-country trading, abandoned general import-export activities in favour of specialisation in particular lines, and diversified into services and manufacturing. The United Africa Company, in particular, was able to draw upon its parent company, Unilever, for technical and managerial expertise [199: *493–508*; 198; 61].

Official enthusiasm for industrial development varied from territory to territory – the administrations in the Gold Coast and Tanganyika, for example, appear to have given it a relatively low priority – but state encouragement by itself was no guarantee of success. Perhaps the most spectacular failure was the ambitious programme in Uganda to industrialise on the basis of cheap electricity from the Owen Falls dam (built at a cost of £13 million). However, few overseas manufacturing firms were attracted into Uganda, the government of which ended up selling much of its electricity to Kenya [130: *130–1*; 107: *235–9*]. In Uganda and Tanganyika in East Africa, as in Nyasaland and Northern Rhodesia in Central Africa, it was discovered that the existence of a common market, access to transport and financial services, and other externalities, favoured the firms in the more established manufacturing centres of Kenya and Southern Rhodesia.

In most colonial territories the acquisition of an industrial sector, however small and however weak its linkages with the rest of the economy, was a major goal of the state's new economic management, valued not just for the additional employment created but for its contribution to the emergence of a rather different social order. As well as diversifying the economy around the primary producing sectors of the early colonial period, post-war governments were seeking to break away from the migratory labour system which such primary production had called into existence. Both as an employer of labour in its own right, especially in the field of transport, and as the manager of the economy as a whole, the colonial state began to promote the 'stabilisation' of labour. A settled proletariat, able to acquire the skills needed for mechanised processes and able to repay employers for the costs of training, became the goal of the new-style labour policy. In Kenya, for example, the Carpenter Report of 1954, which called for the replacement of a minimum wage based upon the single man by one adequate for a family and for more attention to the productivity of labour, merely reflected a shift which was already taking place in official and business thinking [218: *133–9*; 211: *367–75*; 208: *3–59*]. The fact that real wages, depressed for most of the 1930s and 1940s, moved sharply upwards throughout Tropical Africa in the 1950s, partly as a result of trade union activity, was a powerful influence upon employers' practices. In the case of the Northern Rhodesian Copperbelt, the growing power of the African trade unions has been given more credit than the prodding of the local administration for the transition to a permanent or 'stabilised' workforce [210: *202–8*].

The emergence of settled labour in the larger, mainly foreign- and settler-owned mines, plantations and factories, however, did not bring an end to migration out of the areas of peasant cultivation. On the contrary, the relatively high wages paid to workers, together with an urban bias in public expenditure, created a gap between peasant and urban incomes and expectations, which resulted in an exodus of rural youth seeking employment opportunities. At the same time, improvements in labour productivity in the larger public and private establishments reduced their labour requirements. The labour shortages so characteristic of the early colonial period had given way to an abundance of labour.

Demographic change added to the weight of the demand for employment. The true scale, distribution and causes of population growth in colonial Africa remain little known. Official figures suggest that between 1900 and 1960, population in British West Africa grew from about 16 million to about 45 million; in Central Africa from approximately 2 million to over 8 million; and in East Africa (not including Sudan) from 11 million to around 24 million [36: *661*]. The early figures were almost certainly underestimates which exaggerate the scale of change. Nevertheless, demographic growth occurred, at a modest rate (perhaps around 1 per cent) between the wars and at a livelier pace (over 2 per cent) after 1945. A suggestion that the birth rate may have risen in the early colonial period – improvements in income opportunities reducing the age of marriage for men, bringing about a transition from polygamy to monogamy, and producing increased fertility per individual wife [227] – can be regarded as no more than speculative. In the late colonial period (and possibly earlier), the important factor was a fall in the death rate as a consequence of improved transport and food supplies, public health facilities, and wider distribution of modern medicines.

As the demographic dynamic met the rising capital-intensity of the 'modern sector', or the larger capitalist enterprises, there was an expansion of employment in small-scale urban services – what surprised economists would call the 'informal sector' once they had finally discovered it – and also, it would seem, a nascent urban unemployment. At what point the 'modern sector' ceased to grow fast enough to absorb the potential labour force remains open to investigation. In Southern Rhodesia, it is suggested, that point came with the end of the Central African Federation in the 1960s [120], while in Kenya the coincidence of industrial growth with improved productivity in peasant agriculture during the 1950s meant an expanding labour market until after independence, at least. Nevertheless, as British colonialism withdrew between 1955 and

1965, leaving behind only the settler-government of Southern Rhodesia, the economic problems of Tropical Africa were beginning to assume new forms. How to sustain economic growth and development in a situation of low-productivity peasant agriculture, high rates of population growth, and capital-intensive, labour-saving technology in manufacturing, mining and construction, was the problem which the departing colonial governments handed over to their successors.

8 Conclusions

THE preceding pages have attempted to survey what is known, and what has been written, about the economic relationships between Britain and Tropical Africa and about the British impact upon the material life of a major world region. It will have become clear that there is no closely joined debate over the broad contours of these matters. Discussion has been liveliest and most productive, throwing up fresh evidence, pushing forward theoretical perspectives and refining methodological techniques, over what can be termed middle-order problems: the use of the 'vent-for-surplus' model, for example, or the alleged 'proletarianisation' of the African rural societies in settler-dominated economies. New intermediate-tier debates will undoubtedly emerge in the future as part of the shift of historical focus into new areas, like ecology, demography or climatology, and as the archives for the late colonial period begin to open up. But on the upper order questions – how to summarise the colonial period in African economic history – there is more of a mêlée and confusion of purpose than a hard exchange of views on an agenda of agreed issues. The four traditions of scholarship – the imperial, the liberal, the dependency, and the Marxist – whose styles and differing approaches give a flavour and texture to African economic historiography, prove on closer examination to talk, or rather write, past each other more frequently than they engage in dialogue.

The imperial and the dependency 'schools' of thought seem to have had least to contribute to our understanding of Africa's recent economic past. These are traditions of scholarship, almost mirror images of each other, from which doubts are removed and ambiguities erased. A clear message, based upon a careful selection of facts and rejection of those which are inconvenient, can be delivered: colonialism and capitalism *developed* Africa; colonialism and capitalism *underdeveloped* Africa! However, the simple dichotomy between 'development' and 'underdevelopment', like that between 'tradition' and 'modernity' which it replaced in the social sciences, is a trap for the unwary historian, a gap between two ideal types, indeed almost utopian visions of society, which have never existed in the real world. The 'importing of André Gunder Frank' into African scholarship, it would appear, has been an intellectual dead-end, from which some who originally pursued it have subsequently retreated [14]. Tropical Africa certainly became more 'dependent' during the colonial period, its integration into the international economy could have had no other effect, but there is little evidence to support the idea that this brought about an impoverishment of the African peoples. Dependence on external trade and investment, reflecting the difficulty of generating higher productivity within the internal or domestic economy, was more a symptom than a cause of poverty and backwardness.

Liberal and 'classical' Marxist economic historians remain uncertain about their final verdict. They are agreed that production – its scale, its growth, its technology and its social relationships – deserves as much attention as the distribution of the output, or the 'appropriation of surplus': so much so that a convergence in their scholarship may perhaps be perceived. From both traditions has come the view that, despite a deterioration of conditions in some periods and for some people, economic growth occurred in colonial Africa with beneficial effects for most people. For all that growth and welfare were uneven in spread, it was indeed 'Africa's age of improvement' [12]. Nevertheless, the gains are often seen as limited and the impact on Africa's productive capacity less than dramatic. For some, the problem lies in the fact that there was so little development of indigenous capitalism:

> the curious paradox . . . that England, a liberal capitalist society, should have done so little to encourage the emergence of a commercial middle class, and so much to establish a formidable machinery of bureaucratic control. [35: *667*]

For others, it rests on the inability of that machinery to effect any significant increase in the productivity of African agriculture. 'The Nyasaland government', it is claimed, 'made sporadic attempts to bring about a social and economic revolution for which no conditions existed, and which they had neither the resources nor the political will to carry out' [138]. Yet others point to a failure of British capitalism to achieve an effective penetration of African societies, even with the assistance of the colonial state, blaming this on the undercapitalisation of the trading companies and their apparent inability to operate profitably without resort to monopoly [9].

Such conclusions, however, which refer in the main to conditions in 'peasant' economies, sit uneasily alongside views of the colonial state as 'the handmaiden of capitalism' which derive from studies of an economy like Kenya's, with a sizeable settler sector. Such studies focus on factor markets as well as commodity markets, and depict the colonial government as assisting a process of local capital accumulation, mainly by the settler population but also by an African 'petit bourgeoisie' [103; 85; 78; 160]. Generalisations about the intensity of the colonial impact, and the long-run significance of the changes it brought about, must allow for variations from the norm.

That the penetration of British colonialism and capitalism was superficial in most of Tropical Africa cannot be readily dismissed. After all, the period of effective rule was relatively short, not much more than sixty years, within which there occurred two world wars and a major international depression. Given the limited aims of the original territorial annexations, the general lack of interest of British investors in Tropical Africa before the Second World War, and the long-run relative decline of the British economy itself, it is unlikely that any profound transformation would have taken place. Nevertheless, to regard the colonial decades as lacking in innovatory influence and achievement, a kind of static expansion, would be to go too far. Ideas about the 'limited' nature of change too often derive from some unstated ideal situation which was not reached rather than from recognition of extent of departure from an original base-line. Ultimately, therefore, Britain's significance for Tropical Africa can only be assessed by taking account of what had gone before.

Africa's economic backwardness, relative to Europe and Asia, in pre-colonial times has been attributed to a combination of the following factors: (1) a harsh environment, with thin, infertile soils and, over much of the land, slight or irregular rainfall; (2) poor internal transport and communications; (3) low population densities and slow demographic growth, caused by high death rates as well as the export of manpower through the slave trade; and (4) a backward technology of production, resulting in a relative absence of occupational specialisation and lower levels of productivity in agriculture and craft manufacture [4: 8–77; 5: 17–33; 223]. To overcome the disadvantages implicit in the first would necessitate change in the

71

other three. During the first half of the twentieth century, as we have seen, transport facilities had been improved, gradually but cumulatively, by railways, steamers, motor-vehicles and aircraft. A demographic transformation had occurred, on a scale which might truly merit the much abused term 'revolutionary', and what had been a comparatively empty landscape began to fill up. New technologies of production had also been introduced, but far more successfully in some sectors than in others. In small-holder agriculture, which employed the largest share of Africa's land, labour and capital, productivity gains had been made by the introduction of new crops and adjustments in existing techniques and practices rather than by adoption of the new technology and inputs of the industrial age; not just the labour-saving farm machinery, but the artificial fertilisers, pesticides and weed-killers, or the pumps, windmills, small generators and drainage tiles, which had raised per capita output, above all in the crucially important foodcrops, elsewhere in the world. Some of these innovations might not have been immediately appropriate to African conditions, especially in the forest zones, and one must not underestimate the problems of diffusing new methods in rural societies with low rates of literacy. Nevertheless, the absence of any noticeable breakthrough in the productivity of food supply was the biggest gap in the record of the British presence in Tropical Africa, and remains a prime constraint on the growth and development of the African economies.

Bibliography

(Place of publication is London unless otherwise stated)

WORKS OF GENERAL INTEREST

[1]   C. Dewey and A. G. Hopkins, *The Imperial Impact: Studies in The Economic History of Africa and India* (1978).
[2]   P. Duignan and L. H. Gann, *Colonialism in Africa: Vol. 4, The Economics of Colonialism* (Cambridge, 1975).
[3]   L. H. Gann and P. Duignan, *Burden of Empire: An Appraisal of Western Colonialism in Africa South of the Sahara* (New York, 1967).
[4]   A. G. Hopkins, *An Economic History of West Africa* (1973).
[5]   J. F. Munro, *Africa and the International Economy, 1800–1960* (1976).
[6]   W. Rodney, *How Europe Underdeveloped Africa* (1972).

HISTORIOGRAPHY AND THEORETICAL PERSPECTIVES

[7]   E. A. Alpers, 'Rethinking African Economic History', *Kenya Historical Review*, 1 (1973).
[8]   S. Amin, 'Underdevelopment and Dependence in Black Africa', *Journal of Modern African Studies*, 10 (1972).
[9]   R. A. Austen, 'Economic History', *African Studies Review*, 14 (1971).
[10] A. G. Hopkins, 'On Importing André Gunder Frank into Africa', *African Economic History Review*, 2 (1975).
[11] ——, 'Clio-Antics: A Horoscope for African Economic History', in C. Fyfe (ed.), *African Studies Since 1945* (1976).
[12] ——, *Africa's Age of Improvement* (Birmingham, 1980).
[13] G. Kay, *Development and Underdevelopment: A Marxist Analysis* (1975).
[14] C. Leys, 'Underdevelopment and Dependency: Critical Notes', *Journal of Contemporary Asia*, 7 (1977).

[15] I. Phimister, 'Zimbabwean Economic and Social Historiography Since 1970', *African Affairs*, 78 (1979).

[16] D. Rimmer, 'The Economics of Colonialism in Africa', *Journal of African History*, 19 (1978).

[17] B. Warren, *Imperialism: Pioneer of Capitalism* (1980).

THE PARTITION OF AFRICA

[18] J. F. A. Ajayi and R. A. Austen, 'Hopkins on Economic Imperialism in West Africa', *Economic History Review*, 25 (1972).

[19] P. J. Cain, *Economic Foundations of British Expansion Overseas, 1815–1914* (1980).

[20] P. J. Cain and A. G. Hopkins, 'The Political Economy of British Expansion Overseas, 1750–1914' *Economic History Review*, 33 (1980).

[21] N. Etherington, 'Frederick Elton and the South African Factor in the Making of Britain's East African Empire', *Journal of Imperial and Commonwealth History*, 9 (1981).

[22] J. E. Flint, *Sir George Goldie and the Making of Nigeria* (1960).

[23] J. S. Galbraith, *Mackinnon and East Africa* (Cambridge, 1972).

[24] ——, *Crown and Charter: The Early Years of the British South Africa Company* (Berkeley, 1974).

[25] A. G. Hopkins, 'Economic Imperialism in West Africa: Lagos 1880–92', *Economic History Review*, 21 (1968).

[26] W. G. Hynes, *The Economics of Empire: Britain, Africa and the New Imperialism* (1979).

[27] C. Newbury, 'Out of the Pit: The Capital Accumulation of Cecil Rhodes', *Journal of Imperial and Commonwealth History*, 10 (1981).

[28] S. R. Pearson, 'The Economic Imperialism of the Royal Niger Company', *Food Research Institute Studies*, 10 (1971).

[29] I. R. Phimister, 'Rhodes, Rhodesia and the Rand', *Journal of Southern African Studies* (1974).

[30] B. M. Ratcliffe, 'Commerce and Empire: Manchester Merchants and West Africa, 1873–1895', *Journal of Imperial and Commonwealth History*, 7 (1979).

[31] R. Robinson and J. Gallagher, *Africa and the Victorians: The Official Mind of Imperialism*, 2nd ed. (1982).

[32] D. M. Schreuder, *The Scramble for Southern Africa, 1877–1895* (Cambridge, 1980).

[33] C. C. Wrigley, 'Neo-Mercantile Policies and the New Imperialism', in [1].

IMPERIAL AND COLONIAL POLICY

[34] P. T. Bauer, 'Economic Retrospect and Aftermath', in [2].
[35] C. Ehrlich, 'Building and Caretaking: Economic Policy in British Tropical Africa, 1890–1960', *Economic History Review*, 26 (1973).
[36] D. K. Fieldhouse, 'The Economic Exploitation of Africa: Some British and French Comparisons', in P. Gifford and W. R. Louis (eds), *France and Britain in Africa* (New Haven, 1971).
[37] W. K. Hancock, *Survey of British Commonwealth Affairs:* Vol II, *Problems of Economic Policy, 1918–1939* (1940).
[38] S. M. Hardy, 'Joseph Chamberlain and Some Problems of the "Underdeveloped Estates" ', *University of Birmingham Historical Journal*, 11 (1967–68).
[39] A. G. Hopkins, 'The Creation of a Colonial Monetary System: The Origins of the West African Currency Board', *African Historical Studies*, 3 (1970).
[40] R. V. Kubicek, *The Administration of Imperialism: Joseph Chamberlain at the Colonial Office* (Durham, NC, 1969).
[41] J. M. Lee, *Colonial Development and Good Government* (Oxford, 1967).
[42] F. D. Lugard, *The Dual Mandate in British Tropical Africa* (1922).
[43] D. Meredith, 'The British Government and Colonial Economic Policy, 1919–39', *Economic History Review*, 28 (1975).
[44] W. T. Newlyn and D. C. Rowan, *Money and Banking in Colonial Africa* (Oxford, 1954).
[45] B. Niculescu, *Colonial Planning* (1958).
[46] R. Robinson, 'Non-European Foundations of European Imperialism: A Sketch for a Theory of Collaboration', in R. Owen and B. Sutcliffe (eds), *Studies in the Theory of Imperialism* (1972).
[47] S. B. Saul, 'The Economic Significance of Constructive Imperialism', *Journal of Economic History*, 17 (1957).
[48] R. E. Wraith, *Guggisberg* (1967).

EXTERNAL TRADE, INVESTMENT AND BUSINESS

[49] P. T. Bauer, *West African Trade* (Cambridge, 1954).

[50] P. T. Bauer and B. S. Yamey, *Markets, Market Control and Marketing Reform* (1968).

[51] P. N. Davies, *The Trade Makers* (1973).

[52] ——, 'The Impact of the Expatriate Shipping Lines on the Economic Development of British West Africa', *Business History* 19 (1977).

[53] ——, *Sir Alfred Jones: Shipping Entrepreneur Par Excellence* (1978).

[54] A. Emmanuel, *Unequal Exchange* (1972).

[55] S. H. Frankel, *Capital Investment in Africa* (1938).

[56] R. H. Fry, *Bankers in West Africa* (1976).

[57] T. Gregory, *Ernest Oppenheimer and the Economic Development of Southern Africa* (1962).

[58] A. G. Hopkins, 'Imperial Business in Africa: Part 1, Sources; Part 2, Interpretations', *Journal of African History*, 17 (1976).

[59] V. Jamal, 'Asians in Uganda, 1880–1972: Inequality and Expulsion', *Economic History Review*, 29 (1976).

[60] C. Leubuscher, *The West African Shipping Trade* (Leyden, 1963).

[61] R. S. May, 'Direct Overseas Investment in Nigeria, 1953–63', *Scottish Journal of Political Economy*, 12 (1965).

[62] J. S. Mangat, *A History of the Asians of East Africa* (Oxford, 1969).

[63] F. V. Mayer, *Britain's Colonies in the World Trade* (1948).

[64] G. M. Meier, 'External Trade and Internal Development' in [2].

[65] J. F. Milburn, 'The 1938 Gold Coast Cocoa Crisis: British Business and the Colonial Office', *African Historical Studies*, 3 (1970).

[66] ——, *British Businessmen and Ghanaian Independence* (Hanover, N. Hampshire, 1977).

[67] J. Miles, 'Rural Protest in the Gold Coast: The Cocoa Hold-ups, 1908–1938', in [1].

[68] J. F. Munro, 'Monopolists and Speculators: British Investment in West African Rubber, 1905–1914', *Journal of African History*, 22 (1981).

[69] ——, 'British Rubber Companies in East Africa before the First World War', *Journal of African History*, 24 (1983).

[70] C. Newbury, 'Trade and Technology in West Africa: The case of the Niger Company 1900–1920', *Journal of African History*, 19 (1978).

[71] A. I. Nwabughuogu, 'From Wealthy Entrepreneurs to Petty Traders: The Decline of African Middlemen in Eastern Nigeria, 1900–1950', *Journal of African History*, 23 (1982).

[72] F. Pedler, *The Lion and the Unicorn in Africa* (1974).

[73] S. Rhodie, 'The Gold Coast Cocoa Hold-up of 1930–31', *Transactions of the Historical Society of Ghana*, 9 (1968).

[74] J. F. Rweyamamu, 'International Trade and the Developing Countries', *Journal of Modern African Studies*, 7 (1969).

[75] I. R. G. Spencer, 'The First Assault on Indian Ascendancy – Indian Traders in the Kenya Reserves, 1895–1929', *African Affairs*, 80 (1981).

[76] R. Southall, 'Farmers, Traders and Brokers in the Gold Coast Cocoa Economy', *Canadian Journal of African Studies*, 12 (1978).

[77] K. M. Stahl, *The Metropolitan Organization of British Colonial Trade* (1951).

[78] N. Swainson, *The Development of Corporate Capitalism in Kenya, 1918–1977* (1980).

GENERAL STUDIES OF SPECIFIC REGIONS/TERRITORIES

[79] S. Amin, *Neo-Colonialism in West Africa* (Harmondsworth, 1973).

[80] G. Arrighi, *The Political Economy of Rhodesia* (The Hague, 1967).

[81] ——, 'Labour Supplies in Historical Perspective: A Study of the Proletarianization of the African Peasantry in Rhodesia', *Journal of Development Studies*, 6 (1969–70).

[82] R. A. Austen, *Northwest Tanzania under German and British Rule* (New Haven, 1968).

[83] R. E. Baldwin, *Economic Development and Export Growth: A Study of Northern Rhodesia, 1920–1960* (Berkeley, 1966).

[84] W. J. Barber, *The Economy of British Central Africa* (1961).

[85] B. J. Berman and J. M. Lonsdale, 'Crises of Accumulation, Coercion and the Colonial State: The Development of the Labour Control System in Kenya, 1919–1929', *Canadian Journal of African Studies*, 14 (1980).

[86] A. A. Beshai, *Export Performance and Economic Development in the Sudan* (1976).

[87] B. D. Bowles, 'The Political Economy of Colonial Tanganyika, 1939–61', in [99].

[88] E. A. Brett, *Colonialism and Underdevelopment in East Africa* (1973).

[89] C. Ehrlich, 'Some Social and Economic Implications of Paternalism in Uganda', *Journal of African History*, 4 (1963).

[90] ——, 'The Uganda Economy, 1903–1945', in [95].

[91] ——, 'The Poor Country: The Tanganyika Economy from 1945 to Independence', in [105].

[92] C. K. Eicher and C. Liedholm (eds), *Growth and Development of the Nigerian Economy* (East Lansing, 1970).

[93] R. O. Ekundare, *An Economic History of Nigeria* (1973).

[94] L. H. Gann, *A History of Southern Rhodesia: Early Days to 1934* (1965).

[95] V. Harlow and E. M. Chilver (eds), *History of East Africa*, Vol 2 (Oxford, 1965).

[96] R. Howard, *Colonialism and Underdevelopment in Ghana* (1978).

[97] G. Hyden, *Beyond Ujamaa in Tanzania* (1980).

[98] J. Iliffe, *A Modern History of Tanganyika* (Cambridge, 1979).

[99] M. Y. Kaniki, *Tanzania Under Colonial Rule* (1980).

[100] G. B. Kay, *The Political Economy of Colonialism in Ghana* (Cambridge, 1972).

[101] C. Leubuscher, *Tanganika Territory: A Study of Economic Policy under Mandate* (1964).

[102] C. Leys, *Underdevelopment in Kenya* (1975).

[103] J. Lonsdale and B. Berman, 'Coping with Contradiction: The Development of the Colonial State in Kenya, 1895–1914', *Journal of African History*, 20 (1979).

[104] J. Lonsdale, 'Some Origins of Nationalism in East Africa', *Journal of African History*, 9 (1968).

[105] D. A. Low and A. Smith (eds), *History of East Africa*, Vol 3 (Oxford, 1976).

[106] D. A. Low and J. M. Lonsdale, 'Towards the New Order, 1945–1963', in [105].

[107] D. A. Lury, 'Dayspring Mishandled? The Uganda Economy, 1945–1960', in [105].

[108] D. M. P. McCarthy, 'Organising Underdevelopment from the Inside: The Bureaucratic Economy of Tanganyika, 1918–40', *International Journal of African Historical Studies*, 10 (1977).

[109] A. McPhee, *The Economic Revolution in British West Africa* (1926).

[110] M. McWilliam, 'The Managed Economy: Agricultural Change, Development and Finance in Kenya, 1945–1963', in [105].

[111] D. J. Murray, *The Governmental System in Southern Rhodesia* (Oxford, 1970).

[112] M. Perham (ed.), *The Economics of a Tropical Dependency*, 2 vols (1946).

[113] A. Roberts, *A History of Zambia* (1976).

[114] W. Rodney, 'The Political Economy of Tanganyika, 1890–1930', in [99].

[115] P. C. Sederberg, 'The Gold Coast Under Colonial Rule: An Expenditure Analysis', *African Studies Review*, 14 (1971).

[116] R. W. Shenton and W. M. Freund, 'The Incorporation of Northern Nigeria into the World Capitalist Economy', *Review of African Political Economy*, 13 (1978).

[117] M. J. Sibanda, 'Dependency and Underdevelopment in Northwestern Sierra Leone, 1896–1939', *African Affairs*, 78 (1979).

[118] M. P. K. Sorrenson, *Origins of European Settlement in Kenya* (Nairobi, 1968).

[119] I. R. G. Spencer, 'The First World War and the Origins of the Dual Policy of Development in Kenya, 1914–22', *World Development*, 9 (1981).

[120] R. B. Sutcliffe, 'Stagnation and Inequality in Rhodesia: 1946–1968', *Bulletin of the Oxford University Institute of Economics and Statistics*, 33 (1971).

[121] R. Szereszewski, *Structural Changes in the Economy of Ghana, 1891–1911* (1965).

[122] T. F. Taylor, 'The Struggle for Economic Control of Uganda, 1919–22', *International Journal of African Historical Studies*, 11 (1978).

[123] R. D. Wolff, *The Economics of Colonialism: Britain and Kenya, 1870–1930* (New Haven, 1974).

[124] C. C. Wrigley, 'Buganda: An Outline Economic History', *Economic History Review*, 10 (1957–58).

[125] ——, 'Kenya: The Patterns of Economic Life, 1902–1945', in [95].

[126] ——, 'Changes in East African Society', in [105].

[127] C. P. Youé, 'Peasants, Planters and Cotton Capitalists: The Dual Economy in Colonial Uganda', *Canadian Journal of African Studies*, 12 (1978).

[128] ——, 'Colonial Economic Policy in Uganda after World War I: A Re-Assessment', *International Journal of African Historical Studies*, 12 (1978).

[129] R. M. A. Van Zwanenberg, *Colonial Capitalism and Labour in Kenya, 1919–1939* (Nairobi, 1975).

[130] R. M. A. Van Zwanenberg with A. King, *An Economic History of Kenya and Uganda, 1800–1970* (1975).

AGRICULTURE AND AGRARIAN SOCIETIES

[131] W. Allan, *The African Husbandman* (Edinburgh, 1965).
[132] E. S. Atieno-Odiambo, 'The Rise and Decline of the Kenya Peasant, 1888–1922', in P. C. W. Gutkind and P. Waterman (eds), *African Social Studies: A Radical Reader* (1977).
[133] T. Barnett, *The Gezira Scheme: An Illusion of Development* (1977).
[134] S. S. Berry, 'Christianity and the Rise of Cocoa-Growing in Ibadan and Ondo', *Journal of the Historical Society of Nigeria*, 4 (1968).
[135] ——, 'Cocoa and Economic Development in Western Nigeria', in [92].
[136] ——, *Cocoa, Custom and Socio-Economic Change in Rural Western Nigeria* (Oxford, 1975).
[137] L. H. Brown, 'Agricultural Change in Kenya, 1945–1960', *Food Research Institute Studies*, 8 (1968).
[138] M. Chanock, 'Agricultural Change and Continuity in Malawi', in [169].
[139] L. Cliffe, 'Rural Class Formation in East Africa', *Journal of Peasant Studies*, 4 (1977).
[140] F. Cooper, *From Slaves to Squatters: Plantation Labour and Agriculture in Zanzibar and Coastal Kenya, 1890–1925* (New Haven, 1980).
[141] K. Dike Nworah, 'The West African Operations of the British Cotton-Growing Association, 1906–1914', *African Historical Studies*, 4 (1972).
[142] D. C. Dorward, 'An Unknown Nigerian Export: Tiv Benniseed Production, 1900–1960', *Journal of African History*, 16 (1975).
[143] W. R. Duggan, 'The Native Land Husbandry Act of 1951 and the Rural African Middle Class of Southern Rhodesia', *African Affairs*, 79 (1980).
[144] C. H. Elliot, 'Agriculture and Economic Development in Africa', in E. L. Jones and S. L. Woolf (eds), *Agrarian Change and Economic Development* (1969).
[145] A. Gaitskell, *Gezira: A Story of Development in the Sudan* (1959).
[146] I. C. Greaves, *Modern Production among Backward Peoples* (1935).
[147] R. H. Green and S. H. Hymer, 'Cocoa in the Gold Coast: A

Study in Relations between African Farmers and Agricultural Experts', *Journal of Economic History*, 26 (1966).

[148] M. A. Havinden, 'The History of Crop Cultivation in West Africa: A Bibliographical Guide', *Economic History Review*, 23 (1970).

[149] G. K. Helleiner, *Peasant Agriculture, Government and Economic Growth in Nigeria* (Homewood, Ill., 1966).

[150] J. A. Hellen, *Rural Economic Development in Zambia, 1890–1964* (Munich, 1969).

[151] P. Hill, *Migrant Cocoa Farmers of Southern Ghana: A Study in Rural Capitalism* (Cambridge, 1963).

[152] ——, *Studies in Rural Capitalism in West Africa* (Cambridge, 1970).

[153] J. S. Hogendorn, 'The Origins of the Groundnut Trade in Northern Nigeria', in [92].

[154] ——, 'Economic Initiative and African Cash Farming: Pre-Colonial Origins and Early Colonial Developments, in [2].

[155] ——, *Nigerian Groundnut Exports: Origins and Early Development* (Zaria, 1978).

[156] A. G. Hopkins, 'Innovation in a Colonial Context: African Origins of the Nigerian Cocoa-Farming Industry, 1880–1920', in [1].

[157] J. Iliffe, *Agricultural Change in Modern Tanganyika* (Nairobi, 1971).

[158] R. W. M. Johnson, 'African Agricultural Development in Southern Rhodesia, 1945–60', *Food Research Institute Studies*, 4 (1964).

[159] R. W. Kettlewell, 'Agricultural Change in Nyasaland, 1945–60', *Food Research Institute Studies*, 5 (1965).

[160] G. Kitching, *Class and Economic Change in Kenya: The Making of an African Petit Bourgeoisie* (New Haven, 1980).

[161] M. A. Klein, *Peasants in Africa: Historical and Contemporary Perspectives* (1980).

[162] B. Kosmin, 'The Inyoka Tobacco Industry of the Shangwe People: The Displacement of a Pre-Colonial Economy in Southern Rhodesia', in [169].

[163] J. McCracken, 'Re-thinking Rural Poverty', *Journal of African History*, 19 (1978).

[164] S. Makings, 'Agricultural Change in Northern Rhodesia/Zambia, 1945–60', *Food Research Institute Studies*, 6 (1966).

[165] G. B. Masefield, 'Agricultural Change in Uganda, 1945–60', *Food Research Institute Studies*, 3 (1963).

[166] P. Mosley, 'Agricultural Development and Government Policy in Settler Economies: The Case of Kenya and Southern Rhodesia, *Economic History Review*, 35 (1982).

[167] J. F. Munro, *Colonial Rule and the Kamba: Social Change in the Kenya Highlands, 1889–1939* (Oxford, 1975).

[168] M. Mutemba, 'Thwarted Development: A Case Study of Economic Change in the Kabwe Rural District of Zambia, 1902–70', in [169].

[169] R. Palmer and N. Parsons (eds), *The Roots of Rural Poverty in Central and Southern Africa* (1977).

[170] R. Palmer, *Land and Racial Domination in Rhodesia* (1977).

[171] ——, 'The Agricultural History of Rhodesia', in [169].

[172] I. R. Phimister, 'Peasant Production and Underdevelopment in Southern Rhodesia, 1890–1914', *African Affairs*, 73 (1974).

[173] ——, 'Meat and Monopolies: Beef Cattle in Southern Rhodesia, 1890–1938', *Journal of African History*, 19 (1978).

[174] O. B. Pollack, 'Black Farmers and White Politics in Rhodesia', *African Affairs*, 74 (1975).

[175] T. Ranger, 'Growing from the Roots: Reflections on Peasant Research in Central and Southern Africa: *Journal of Southern African Studies*, 5 (1978).

[176] J. K. Rennie, 'White Farmers, Black Tenants and Landlord Legislation: Southern Rhodesia, 1890–1930', *Journal of Southern African Studies*, 5 (1978).

[177] A. I. Richards, F. Sturrock and J. M. Forts (eds), *Subsistence to Commercial Farming in Present Day Buganda* (Cambridge, 1974).

[178] L. D. Smith, 'An Overview of Agricultural Development Policy', in J. Heyer, J. K. Maitha and W. M. Senga (eds), *Agricultural Development in Kenya* (Nairobi, 1976).

[179] M. P. K. Sorrenson, *Land Reform in Kikuyu Country* (1967).

[180] I. R. G. Spencer, 'Settler Dominance, Agricultural Production and the Second World War in Kenya', *Journal of African History*, 21 (1980).

[181] J. Tosh, 'Lango Agriculture During the Early Colonial Period', *Journal of African History*, 19 (1978).

[182] ——, 'The Cash Crop Revolution in Tropical Africa: An Agricultural Reappraisal', *African Affairs*, 79 (1980).

[183] R. M. A. Van Zwanenberg, *The Agricultural History of Kenya* (Nairobi, 1972).

[184] ——, 'The Development of Peasant Commodity Production in Kenya, 1920–1940', *Economic History Review*, 27 (1974).

[185] M. Vaughan, 'Food Production and Family Labour in Southern Malawi', *Journal of African History*, 23 (1982).

[186] A. R. Waters, 'Change and Evolution in the Kenya Coffee Industry', *African Affairs*, 71 (1972).

[187] C. C. Wrigley, *Crops and Wealth in Uganda: A Short Agrarian History* (Kampala, 1959).

INTERNAL TRANSPORT, MINING AND MANUFACTURING

[188] P. Y. Bauer and B. S. Yamey, 'Industrialization and Development – The Nigerian Experience', *Economic History Review*, 25 (1972).

[189] F. L. Coleman, *The Northern Rhodesia Copperbelt, 1899–1962* (Manchester, 1971).

[190] A. H. Croxton, *Railways of Rhodesia* (Newton Abbot, 1973).

[191] W. M. Freund, 'Labour Migration to the Northern Nigerian Tin Mines, 1902–1945', *Journal of African History*, 22 (1981).

[192] ——, *Capital and Labour in the Nigerian Tin Mines* (1981).

[193] L. H. Gann, 'The Northern Rhodesian Copper Industry and the World of Copper, 1923–52', *Rhodes-Livingstone Journal*, 18 (1955).

[194] P. R. Gould, *The Development of the Transportation Pattern in Ghana* (Evanston, Ill., 1960).

[195] M. F. Hill, *Permanent Way: The Story of the Kenya and Uganda Railway* (Nairobi, 1950).

[196] M. Johnston, 'Cotton Imperialism in West Africa', *African Affairs*, 73 (1974).

[197] ——, 'Technology, Competition and African Crafts', in [1].

[198] P. Kilby, *Industrialization in an Open Economy: Nigeria, 1945–1966* (Cambridge, 1969).

[199] ——, 'Manufacturing in Colonial Africa', in [2].

[200] G. Lanning and M. Mueller, *Africa Undermined: Mining Companies and the Underdevelopment of Africa* (Harmondsworth, 1979).

[201] O. Omosini, 'Railway Projects and British Attitudes towards the Development of West Africa, 1872–1903', *Journal of the Historical Society of Nigeria*, 5 (1971).

[202] W. Oyemakinde, 'Rail Construction and Operation in Nigeria, 1895–1911', *Journal of Historical Society of Nigeria*, 7 (1974).

[203] I. R. Phimister, 'The Reconstruction of the Southern Rhodesian Gold Mining Industry, 1903–10', *Economic History Review*, 29 (1976).

[204] J. Silver, 'The Failure of European Mining Companies in the Nineteenth Century Gold Coast', *Journal of African History*, 22 (1981).

[205] P. Slinn, 'Commercial Concessions and Politics During the Colonial Period: The Role of the British South Africa Company in Northern Rhodesia, 1890–1964', *African Affairs*, 70 (1971).

[206] I. B. Sutton, 'The Volta River Salt Trade: The Survival of an Indigenous Industry', *Journal of African History*, 22 (1981).

[207] L. Vail, 'The Making of an Imperial Slum: Nyasaland and its Railways, 1895–1935', *Journal of African History*, 16 (1975).

Labour

[208] A. H. Amsden, *International Firms and Labour in Kenya, 1945–1970* (1971).

[209] E. J. Berg, 'The Development of a Labour Force in Sub-Saharan Africa', *Economic Development and Cultural Change*, 12 (1965).

[210] E. Berger, *Labour, Race and Colonial Rule: The Copperbelt from 1924 to Independence* (Oxford, 1974).

[211] A. Clayton and D. C. Savage, *Government and Labour in Kenya, 1893–1963* (1974).

[212] J. Iliffe, 'Wage Labour and Urbanisation', in [99].

[213] M. Mason, 'Working on the Railway: Forced Labour in Northern Nigeria, 1907–12', in P. Gutkind, R. Cohen and J. Copans (eds), *African Labour History* (1978).

[214] M. P. Miracle and B. Fetter, 'Backward-Sloping Labour Supply Functions and African Economic Behaviour', *Economic Development and Cultural Change*, 18 (1970).

[215] C. W. Newbury, 'Labour Migration in the Imperial Phase: An Essay in Interpretation', *Journal of Imperial and Commonwealth History*, 3 (1975).

[216] —, 'Historical Aspects of Manpower and Migration in Africa South of the Sahara', in [2].

[217] R. Sandbrook and R. Cohen, *The Development of an African Working Class* (1975).

[218] S. Stichter, *Migrant Labour in Kenya: Capitalism and African Response, 1895–1975* (1982).

[219] R. G. Thomas, 'Forced Labour in British West Africa: The Case of the Northern Territories of the Gold Coast, 1906–1927', *Journal of African History*, 14 (1973).

[220] C. Van Onselen, 'Worker Consciousness in Black Miners: Southern Rhodesia, 1900–20', *Journal of African History*, 14 (1973).

[221] ——, *Chibaro: African Mine Labour in Southern Rhodesia* (1976).

OTHER TOPICS

[222] E. A. Alpers, *Ivory and Slaves in East Central Africa* (1975).

[223] J. Goody, *Technology, Tradition and the State in Africa* (1971).

[224] R. Gray and D. Birmingham (eds), *Pre-Colonial African Trade* (1970).

[225] G. W. Hartwig, 'Social Consequences of Epidemic Diseases: The Nineteenth Century in Eastern Africa', in G. W. Hartwig and K. D. Patterson (eds), *Disease in African History* (Durham, NC, 1978).

[226] C. V. Ilegbune, 'Concessions Scramble and Land Alienation in British Southern Ghana, 1885–1916', *African Studies Review*, 29 (1976).

[227] G. Kitching, 'Proto-Industrialization and Demographic Change: A Thesis and Some Possible African Implications', *Journal of African History*, 24 (1983).

[228] H. Kjekshus, *Ecology Control and Economic Development in East African History* (1977).

[229] R. R. Kuczynski, *Demographic Survey of the British Colonial Empire*, Vols 1–2 (1949).

[230] J. McCracken, 'Experts and Expertise in Colonial Malawi', *African Affairs*, 81 (1982).

[231] C. Van Onselen, 'Reactions to Rinderpest in Southern Africa, 1896–97', *Journal of African History*, 13 (1972).

[232] B. Ingham, *Tropical Exports and Economic Development* (1981).

[233] P. Mosley, *The Settler Economies: Studies in the Economic History of Kenya and Southern Rhodesia, 1900–1963* (Cambridge, 1983).

Index